Principles of Cost Accounting

Twelfth Edition

Edward J. VanDerbeck

Xavier University

SOUTH-WESTERN

THOMSON LEARNING

Australia · Canada · Mexico · Singapore · Spain · United Kingdom · United States

Study Guide to accompany Principles of Cost Accounting, 12e
by Edward J. VanDerbeck

Publisher: Melissa S. Acuña
Acquisitions Editor: Jennifer L. Codner
Developmental Editor: Ken Martin and Bari Shokler
Marketing Manager: Larry Qualls
Production Editor: Heather Mann
Manufacturing Coordinator: Doug Wilke
Production Services: Cover to Cover Publishing, Inc.; Gail Strietmann
Printer: Globus Printing, Inc.

Printed in the United States of America
3 4 5 04 03

For more information contact South-Western College Publishing, 5191 Natorp Blvd., Mason, Ohio, 45040 or find us on the Internet at http://www.swcollege.com
For permission to use material from this text or product, contact us by
• telephone: 1-800-730-2214
• fax: 1-800-730-2215
• web: http://www.thomsonrights.com

ISBN: 0-324-10884-2

CHAPTER 1 INTRODUCTION TO COST ACCOUNTING

Review Summary

1. The function of **cost accounting** is to provide the detailed cost data essential to management in controlling current operations and planning for the future. The information systems of manufacturing companies must be designed to accumulate this detailed cost data relating to the production process. While the cost accounting systems illustrated in the text mostly pertain to manufacturers, many of the same principles apply to merchandising and service businesses. Cost accounting systems show what costs were incurred and how they were used.

2. Cost accounting procedures provide the means to determine product costs and thus to generate meaningful financial statements and management reports. The cost procedures must be designed to permit the determination of **unit costs** as well as total costs. Unit costs are also useful in making a variety of marketing decisions such as determining the selling price of a product, deciding how to meet competition, arriving at a contract bid price, and analyzing profitability.

3. One of the most important functions of cost accounting is the development of information that can be used in planning and controlling operations. **Planning** is the process of selecting goals and objectives and determining the means by which they will be attained. Cost accounting aids planning by providing historical costs that can be used to estimate future costs and operating results and to decide whether to acquire additional facilities, change marketing strategies, and obtain capital. **Control** is the process of monitoring the company's operations and determining whether the plans are being accomplished. Effective control is achieved by: assigning accountability for costs to individuals who have the authority to influence them; periodically measuring operating results and comparing them to the plan; and taking necessary corrective action when the operating results deviate from the plan.

4. **Financial accounting** focuses on the gathering of information for use in the preparation of financial statements for external users. **Cost accounting** is used to determine cost of goods sold on the income statement, to determine inventory valuation on the balance sheet, and to prepare special reports for company management. A manufacturer computes **cost of goods sold** by adding cost of goods manufactured to beginning finished goods inventory and then subtracting ending finished goods inventory. The balance sheet for a manufacturer includes the following three inventory accounts:

   Finished goods—Its balance represents the cost to manufacture goods completed but still on hand.
   Work in process—Its balance includes the manufacturing costs to date for unfinished goods.
   Materials—Its balance contains the cost of all materials purchased and still on hand.

5. The three elements of manufacturing cost include direct materials, direct labor, and factory overhead. **Direct materials** are materials that become a readily identifiable part of the item being manufactured. **Direct labor** is the cost of labor for those employees

who work directly on converting the raw materials to finished goods. **Factory overhead** includes indirect materials, indirect labor, and all other manufacturing costs incurred in production but not identifiable directly with a specific product. **Prime cost** equals the combined cost of direct materials and direct labor; **conversion cost** equals the sum of direct labor plus factory overhead.

6. The following journal entries are basic to manufacturing accounting:

(a) Materials XX
     Accounts Payable XX
       Purchased materials.

(b) Work in Process (Direct Materials) XX
   Factory Overhead (Indirect Materials) XX
     Materials XX
       Issued direct and indirect materials into production.

(c) Payroll XX
     Wages Payable XX
   Wages Payable XX
     Cash XX
       Recorded and paid payroll.

(d) Work in Process (Direct Labor) XX
   Factory Overhead (Indirect Labor) XX
   Selling and Administrative Expenses (Salaries) XX
     Payroll XX
       Distributed payroll.

(e) Factory Overhead XX
     Accounts Payable XX
     Accumulated Depreciation XX
     Prepaid Insurance XX
       Recognized various factory overhead expenses for period.

(f) Work in Process XX
     Factory Overhead XX
       Transferred balance in factory overhead to work in process.

(g) Finished Goods XX
     Work in Process XX
       Transferred cost of goods completed.

(h) Cost of Goods Sold XX
     Finished Goods XX
       Transferred cost of goods sold.

7. To provide management with the data needed for effective cost control, two types of cost accounting systems have been developed—process cost and job order cost. A **process cost system** generally is used when a manufacturer maintains a continuous output of homogeneous products for stock such as cement and chemicals. A **job order cost system** is used when the output consists of special or custom-made products such as books or furniture. In a process cost system, costs are accumulated by department or process, whereas in a job order cost system they are accumulated by job or lot. Some companies' costing systems utilize elements of both job order and process costing. A **standard cost system** may be used with either a job order or process cost system and focuses on **standard costs** that would be incurred under the most efficient operating

conditions. **Variances** represent differences between actual costs and standard costs and aid management in identifying and eliminating inefficient operating conditions.

Part I

Instructions: Indicate your answer in the Answers column by writing a "T" for True or an "F" for False.

Answers

1. The function of cost accounting is to provide the detailed cost data needed to control current operations and plan for the future. .... _____

2. Most service businesses do not need structured cost accounting systems. .... _____

3. Cost procedures must be designed to permit the determination of unit costs as well as total product costs. .... _____

4. Cost accounting aids in the development of plans by providing historical costs that serve as a basis for projecting data for planning. .... _____

5. Under responsibility accounting, the manager of a department is responsible only for those costs that the manager controls...................... _____

6. Current operations may be considered well-managed if the results are better than the budget for the period.. _____

7. To compute cost of goods sold for a manufacturing firm, add ending finished goods inventory to cost of goods manufactured and subtract beginning finished goods inventory... _____

8. A manufacturer has three major types of inventory. .... _____

9. Under a perpetual inventory system, inventory valuation data for financial statement purposes are available at any time. .... _____

10. Direct labor cost usually includes payroll related costs, such as group insurance and sick pay... _____

11. Manufacturing costs usually include selling and administrative expenses... _____

12. Direct materials, direct labor, and factory overhead all flow through the work in process inventory account. .... _____

13. The wages earned by the factory supervisor and the maintenance personnel are charged to Factory Overhead as direct labor.......................... _____

14. Industries that would be most apt to use job order costing include cement and beverage manufacturers. .... _____

15. Standard costs are those costs that would be incurred under efficient operating conditions.. _____

Part II

Instructions: In the Answers column, place the letter from the list below that identifies the term that best matches the statement. No letter should be used more than once.

a. Control
b. Periodic inventory system
c. Conversion cost
d. Cost center
e. Job order cost accounting system
f. Factory ledger
g. Factory overhead

h. Manufacturing process
i. Indirect materials
j. Responsibility accounting
k. Standard cost accounting system
l. Financial accounting
m. Prime cost

n. Job cost sheet
o. Mark-on percentage
p. Cost accounting
q. Planning
r. Process cost accounting system
s. Direct materials
t. Performance report

Answers

_____ 1. This provides the detailed cost data that are essential to management in controlling current operations and planning for the future.

_____ 2. This involves the conversion of raw materials into finished goods through the application of labor and the incurrence of various factory expenses.

_____ 3. The process of selecting goals and objectives and determining the means by which they will be attained.

_____ 4. The process of monitoring operations and determining whether the objectives identified in the planning process are being accomplished.

_____ 5. The assignment of accountability for costs or production results to those individuals who have the authority to influence them.

_____ 6. A unit of activity within the factory to which costs may be practically and equitably assigned.

_____ 7. This should include only those cost and production data that are controllable by the center's manager.

_____ 8. This focuses upon the gathering of information used in the preparation of financial statements for external users.

_____ 9. This requires estimating inventories during the year when interim statements are prepared.

_____ 10. This contains all of the accounts relating to manufacturing, including the inventory accounts.

_____ 11. These become part of the item manufactured and can be readily identified with the item.

_____ 12. This is a term used to describe the combined cost of direct materials and direct labor.

_____ 13. This is a term used to describe the combined cost of direct labor and factory overhead.

_____ **14.** This is added to the manufacturing cost to cover the product's share of selling and administrative expenses and to earn a satisfactory profit.

_____ **15.** A manufacturing system characterized by final products that are substantially identical across all units and by a production process that involves turning out units for stock.

_____ **16.** A manufacturing system characterized by an output of special or custom-made products.

_____ **17.** All of the costs applicable to a job will be accumulated on this form.

_____ **18.** These include sandpaper, lubricants, and other items meant for general factory use.

_____ **19.** An accounting system in which costs are charged to inventory accounts at the amounts that should have been incurred for the period rather than the amounts that were incurred.

_____ **20.** It includes all costs related to the manufacture of a product except direct materials and direct labor.

Part III

Instructions: In the Answers column, place the letter of the choice that most correctly completes each item.

Answers

_____ **1.** Work in Process is debited and Materials is credited for a:
   a. Purchase of goods on account
   b. Transfer of completed production to the finished goods storeroom
   c. Transfer of completed goods out of the factory
   d. Transfer of direct materials to the factory

_____ **2.** Predetermined costs for direct materials, direct labor, and factory overhead established by using information accumulated from past experience and scientific research are:
   a. Budgets   c. Normal costs
   b. Actual costs   d. Standard costs

_____ **3.** Inventoriable costs are:
   a. Manufacturing costs incurred to produce units of output
   b. All costs associated with manufacturing, other than direct labor and raw materials
   c. Costs associated with marketing, shipping, warehousing, and billing
   d. The sum of direct labor and all factory overhead

_____ **4.** The best cost accumulation system to use when a manufacturer maintains a continuous mass production of like units is:
   a. Actual costing   c. Job order costing
   b. Standard costing   d. Process costing

5. An industry that would most likely use process costing procedures is:
   a. Printing
   b. Beverage
   c. Shipbuilding
   d. Machine tools

6. A typical factory overhead cost is:
   a. Direct materials
   b. Shipping
   c. Depreciation on the plant
   d. Direct labor

7. Finished Goods is debited and Work in Process is credited for a:
   a. Purchase of goods on account
   b. Transfer of completed production to the finished goods storeroom
   c. Transfer of completed goods out of the factory
   d. Transfer of materials to the factory

8. The gross profit of Crowe Company for the year is $150,000, cost of goods manufactured is $500,000, the beginning inventory of finished goods is $25,000, and the ending inventory of finished goods is $50,000. Compute the sales of Crowe Company for the year. (Hint: First determine cost of goods sold.)
   a. $675,000
   b. $650,000
   c. $625,000
   d. $525,000

9. For the year, the sales of Software Inc. were $323,000; the cost of goods manufactured was $260,000; the beginning inventories of work in process and finished goods were $25,000 and $40,000, respectively; and the ending inventories of work in process and finished goods were $15,000 and $32,000, respectively. Compute the gross profit of Software Inc. for the year:
   a. $60,000
   b. $45,000
   c. $55,000
   d. $50,000

10. Unit cost information is useful for all of the following except:
    a. Determining the selling price of a product
    b. Bidding on contracts
    c. Achieving responsibility accounting
    d. Analyzing profitability

Name _____

Part IV

Instructions: Place a check mark in the appropriate column to indicate the proper classification of each of the following costs.

Item	Indirect Materials	Indirect Labor	Other Indirect Manufacturing Costs	Selling and Administrative Expenses
1. Accounting fees................	_____	_____	_____	_____
2. Factory lease....................	_____	_____	_____	_____
3. Lubricants.......................	_____	_____	_____	_____
4. Supervision.....................	_____	_____	_____	_____
5. Administrative salaries.....	_____	_____	_____	_____
6. Uncollectible accounts expense.........................	_____	_____	_____	_____
7. Shipping..........................	_____	_____	_____	_____
8. Samples of new products .	_____	_____	_____	_____
9. Payroll taxes on factory wages..............................	_____	_____	_____	_____
10. Factory heat, light, and power..............................	_____	_____	_____	_____
11. Overtime premium for factory workers................	_____	_____	_____	_____
12. Experimental work by engineers.........................	_____	_____	_____	_____
13. Glue and nails in finished product.........................	_____	_____	_____	_____
14. Cleaning compound for factory.............................	_____	_____	_____	_____
15. Sales commissions	_____	_____	_____	_____
16. Depreciation on manu-facturing plant	_____	_____	_____	_____
17. Legal fees........................	_____	_____	_____	_____
18. Depreciation on general office building	_____	_____	_____	_____
19. Wages of factory store-room clerk	_____	_____	_____	_____
20. Idle time due to assembly line breakdown...............	_____	_____	_____	_____

Part V

Instructions: Record the correct debit(s) and credit(s) for each of the following transactions, selecting the appropriate letter(s) from the list of account titles.

a. Finished Goods
b. Cost of Goods Sold
c. Income Summary
d. Materials
e. Payroll
f. Factory Overhead
g. Work in Process
h. Selling and Administrative Expenses

i. Cash
j. Accounts Payable
k. Accumulated Depreciation
l. Prepaid Insurance
m. Accounts Receivable
n. Sales
o. Wages Payable

Transactions	Debit	Credit
1. Purchased materials on account	_____	_____
2. Returned some of the materials in (1) to the vendor	_____	_____
3. Paid for the remainder of the materials in (1)	_____	_____
4. Issued direct materials and indirect materials from the storeroom	_____	_____
5. Recorded payroll, ignoring payroll deductions	_____	_____
6. Paid the payroll	_____	_____
7. Distributed the payroll, which consisted of direct labor, indirect labor, and sales salaries	_____	_____
8. Recorded depreciation on the building that houses both the factory and the general offices	_____	_____
9. Paid the premium in advance on a three-year insurance policy on factory equipment	_____	_____
10. Prepared an adjusting entry for the expired portion of the insurance in (9)	_____	_____
11. Received the monthly utility bill related to plant and general office usage	_____	_____
12. Factory overhead was transferred to the work in process account	_____	_____
13. Completed all jobs that were started in process	_____	_____
14. Shipped various jobs to customers on account	_____	_____

Name _____

Part VI

The following data relate to Harvey Company:

	Inventories	
	Ending	**Beginning**
Work in Process	$20,000	$25,000
Materials	10,000	15,000

Costs incurred during the period:

Purchases...	$22,000
Indirect materials	3,000
Direct labor	30,000
Indirect labor	8,000
Other factory overhead	7,500

Instructions: Prepare a statement of cost of goods manufactured for Harvey Company for the year ended December 31, 2001.

CHAPTER 2 ACCOUNTING FOR MATERIALS

Review Summary

1. **Materials control** includes physical control of materials and control of the investment in materials. Effective physical control of materials involves limiting the access to stored materials, segregating the duties of employees who handle materials and materials reports, and establishing an accurate recording system for materials purchases and issues. Only authorized personnel should be permitted in material storage areas, and procedures for moving materials into and out of these areas should be well established. The following functions of materials control should be segregated to minimize opportunities for employee misappropriation: purchasing, receiving, storage, use, and recording. To ensure the accurate recording of purchases and materials issues, inventory records should document the determination of inventory quantities on hand, and cost records should provide the data for the valuation of inventories to be used in the preparation of financial statements.

2. Controlling the materials inventory investment requires analysis and planning to determine when orders should be placed and the number of units to be ordered. The point at which the predetermined minimum level of inventory is reached, requiring the item to be ordered, is called the **order point**. Establishing order points requires consideration of the following:

   Usage—The anticipated rate at which the materials will be used.
   Lead time—The estimated time interval between placing the order and receiving the materials ordered.
   Safety stock—The estimated minimum level of inventory needed to protect against **stockouts**.

   The order point can be calculated as follows:

   $$(\text{Expected Daily Usage} \times \text{Lead Time}) + \text{Safety Stock}$$

3. The optimal quantity of materials to order at one time, called the **economic order quantity**, is the order size that minimizes the total order and carrying costs. **Order costs** include salaries and wages, communication costs, and recordkeeping. **Carrying costs** include storage and handling; interest, insurance, and property taxes; and losses due to theft, spoilage, or obsolescence. Annual order costs decrease when order size increases while annual carrying costs increase with increases in order size. The economic order quantity formula is:

   $$\sqrt{\frac{2 \times (\text{cost of placing an order})(\text{annual number of units required})}{(\text{carrying cost per unit})}}$$

   The economic order quantity is the point where total order costs equal total carrying costs unless there is a provision for safety stock.

4. Materials control personnel include (a) the **purchasing agent** who is responsible for purchasing the materials needed at the most economical price; (b) the **receiving clerk** who is responsible for supervising incoming shipments of material; (c) the storeroom keeper who is responsible for storing and maintaining the goods received; and (d) the

production department supervisor who is responsible for supervising the operations of a particular department.

5. The supporting documents used in the procurement process include (a) the **purchase requisition**, which is prepared by the storeroom keeper to notify the purchasing agent that additional materials should be ordered; (b) the **purchase order**, which is prepared by the purchasing agent describing the materials ordered, stating terms and prices, and fixing the date and method of delivery; (c) the **vendor's invoice**, which the purchasing agent compares to the purchase order to verify description of materials, price, terms of payment, method of shipment, and delivery date; (d) the **receiving report**, which is prepared by the receiving clerk who counts and identifies the materials received and records the shipper, the date of receipt, the materials received, and the number of the purchase order identifying the shipment; and (e) the **debit-credit memorandum**, which is prepared when the type, quantity, or quality of goods ordered differs from that which was shipped and adjustments must be made to the vendor's invoice. If goods are to be returned, the purchasing agent will prepare a **return shipping order**.

6. After materials have been ordered, received, and transferred to the storeroom, they must be protected from unauthorized use. Materials should not be issued from the storeroom without written authorization in the form of a properly approved **materials requisition**. Occasionally materials are returned to the storeroom because, for example, more materials were requisitioned than were actually needed for production or perhaps the wrong type of material was issued. Returned materials should be accompanied by a **returned materials report**.

7. All purchases of material should be recorded in the general ledger as a debit to Materials. The materials account is a control account supported by a subsidiary **stores ledger**. The individual accounts in the stores ledger are designed to show the quantity of each material on hand and its cost. When materials receipts and issues are posted to the stores ledger accounts, the balance is extended after each entry so that it may be determined when stock is falling below minimum requirements.

8. There are several acceptable ways of assigning costs to materials as they are issued. Under the **first-in, first-out (FIFO)** method of costing, the materials issued are costed at the earliest prices paid for the materials in stock and the ending inventories are costed at the most recent purchase prices. Under the **last-in, first-out (LIFO)** method of costing, the materials issued are costed at the most recent purchase prices and the ending inventories are costed at the prices paid for the earliest purchases. Under the **moving average method** an average unit price is computed each time a new lot of materials is received, and the new unit price is used to cost all issues until another lot is received and a new unit price is computed. In choosing an inventory costing method, the method selected should accurately reflect the income for the period, in terms of current economic conditions. Under conditions of rising prices the LIFO method is often selected because the higher priced materials are charged against the increasingly higher sales revenue, resulting in a more representative earnings picture and a lower income tax liability. When prices stabilize, many companies return to the FIFO method, which is simpler and less expensive clerically and which fairly depicts profits under stable price conditions. Many companies have adopted the middle-of-the-road position represented by the moving average method, especially now that computer programs do the computations.

9. All materials issued to production and those returned to stock during a period are recorded on a **summary of materials issued and returned.** At the end of the period, the summary provides the information necessary to record the cost of materials. The total cost of direct materials requisitioned is recorded by debiting Work in Process and crediting Materials. The total cost of indirect materials requisitioned is recorded by debiting the appropriate factory overhead account and crediting materials. Unused materials returned from the factory to the storeroom are recorded by debiting Materials and crediting Work in Process (direct materials) or Factory Overhead (indirect materials). Any materials returned to vendors should be recorded by debiting Accounts Payable and crediting Materials.

10. **Scrap** or **waste materials** may result from the production process. If the expected sales revenue from scrap is small, no entry is made for the scrap material until it is sold. At the time of sale, Cash or Accounts Receivable is debited and Scrap Revenue, Work in Process, or Factory Overhead is credited depending on whether or not the scrap can be identified with a specific job or department. If the revenue from scrap is expected to be substantial, Scrap Material should be debited and Scrap Revenue should be credited at the time the scrap is inventoried. **Spoiled units** are imperfect units of the primary product and have a defect that cannot be economically corrected. The spoiled goods should be recorded in an inventory account at the expected sales value in one of the two following ways:

Spoiled Goods Inventory	XX	
Factory Overhead	XX	
Work in Process		XXXX
If charging the unrecovered costs of spoilage to factory overhead.		

OR

Spoiled Goods Inventory	XX	
Work in Process		XX
If charging the loss due to spoilage to a specific job.		

Defective units have an imperfection which is considered correctable at an additional cost. When defective work results from regular production, the costs of correcting the defects are charged to factory overhead, but when defective work results from special orders, the rework cost is charged to the order. The entries follow:

Factory Overhead	XXXX	
Materials		XX
Payroll		XX
Factory Overhead		XX
When the cost of the defects results from regularly produced goods.		

OR

Work in Process	XXXX	
Materials		XX
Payroll		XX
Factory Overhead		XX
When the defects result from a special order.		

11. A **just-in-time inventory system** significantly reduces inventory carrying costs by requiring that raw materials be delivered only when they are ready to be used and by eliminating inventory buffers of raw materials between work centers.

Name _____

Part I

Instructions: Indicate your answer in the Answers column by writing a "T" for True or an "F" for False.

Answers

1. Effective control of materials involves limiting the access to stored materials, segregating the duties of employees who handle materials and materials reports, and establishing an accurate recording system for materials purchases and issues... _____

2. The assignment of different personnel to the functions of purchasing, receiving, storage, use, and recording of materials reduces the danger of misappropriation. .... _____

3. The time at which an item should be ordered usually is referred to as the economic order quantity... _____

4. The safety stock protects against inaccurate estimates of usage, lead time variances, and other unforeseen events. .... _____

5. Annual order costs increase when order size increases while annual carrying costs decrease with increases in order size. .... _____

6. When no safety stock is present, the EOQ is usually at the point where total ordering costs exactly equal total carrying costs............................... _____

7. The responsibility of supervising all functions relating to an incoming shipment of materials usually is assigned to the receiving clerk. .... _____

8. The purchase requisition usually originates with the storeroom keeper... _____

9. The materials shipped by the vendor should arrive at the factory receiving dock prior to the receipt of the vendor's invoice. .... _____

10. When goods are returned to the vendor the buyer prepares a debit memorandum. .... _____

11. Materials is a control account supported by a subsidiary stores ledger. ... _____

12. When materials receipts and issues are posted to the stores ledger accounts, the balance is extended after each entry................................... _____

13. The prices paid for the most recent purchases are used to cost the ending inventory when the FIFO method is used.. _____

14. If rework to correct defective units resulted from the exacting specifications of the order, Factory Overhead should be debited for the cost of the rework... _____

15. If materials on hand are less than the control account balance, Factory Overhead should be debited and Materials credited for the difference.... _____

Part II

Instructions: In the Answers column, place the letter from the list below that identifies the term that best matches the statement. No letter should be used more than once.

a. Purchase order
b. Receiving report
c. Velocity
d. Production department supervisor
e. Economic order quantity
f. Returned materials report

g. FIFO
h. Defective units
i. Nonvalue added activities
j. Spoiled units
k. LIFO
l. Just-in-time inventory system

m. Stores ledger
n. Stores requisition
o. Order point
p. Trigger points
q. Debit memorandum
r. Receiving clerk
s. Safety stock
t. Purchase requisition

Answers

_____ 1. It is here that the predetermined minimum level of inventory for an item has been reached.

_____ 2. The estimated minimum level of inventory needed to protect against running out of stock.

_____ 3. In determining this, consideration must be given to the costs of placing an order and the costs of carrying inventories in stock.

_____ 4. Indicate when journal entries are recorded in a backflush costing system.

_____ 5. Responsible for checking orders against shipments for quantity and quality of goods.

_____ 6. Duties include the preparation of materials requisitions and designating the kind and quality of materials needed.

_____ 7. It is used to notify the purchasing agent that additional materials should be ordered.

_____ 8. It describes the materials ordered, stating prices and terms, and fixing the date and method of delivery.

_____ 9. It shows the shipper, the date of receipt, the materials received, and the number of the purchase order that identifies the shipment.

_____ 10. A measure of the speed with which units are produced in a manufacturing system.

_____ 11. This is prepared when the materials shipped do not meet the buyer's specifications and when the materials are going to be returned.

_____ 12. This is originated by factory personnel who have been authorized to withdraw materials from the stockroom.

_____ 13. This should be prepared after an order is started in the factory and it is discovered that more materials were issued than are needed for the job.

_____ 14. This supports the materials control account in the general ledger.

_____ 15. This method of inventory costing assigns the oldest prices to the materials issued.

_____ 16. It significantly reduces inventory carrying costs by requiring that raw materials be delivered only when they are ready to be used and by eliminating inventory buffers of raw materials between work centers.

_____ 17. Under conditions of rising prices this method of inventory costing is selected to minimize income taxes.

_____ 18. These are operations that include costs but do not enhance the product.

_____ 19. These have an imperfection that cannot be corrected economically.

_____ 20. These have an imperfection that is considered correctable at an additional cost.

Part III

Instructions: In the Answers column, place the letter of the choice that most correctly completes each item.

Answers

_____ 1. When spoilage occurs as a result of exacting specifications or difficult processing, any loss is charged to:
   a. Extraordinary losses
   b. The specific job in which the spoilage occurred
   c. Administrative expenses
   d. Factory overhead control

_____ 2. The inventory method that assumes that the cost of the most recently purchased merchandise or materials are assignable to inventory is:
   a. Average costing   c. Next-in, first-out costing
   b. LIFO costing   d. FIFO costing

_____ 3. If inventory prices are stable or increasing, an argument which is not in favor of the LIFO method as compared to FIFO is:
   a. Income tax tends to be reduced in periods of rising prices
   b. Cost of goods sold tends to be stated at approximately current cost in the income statement
   c. Cost assignments typically parallel the physical flow of goods
   d. Income tends to be smoothed as prices change over a period of time

_____ 4. A company's balance sheet inventory cost using FIFO was higher than LIFO. Assuming no beginning inventory, the direction of movement of the cost of purchases during the period was:
   a. Up   c. Steady
   b. Down   d. Undeterminable

5. The Collins Company requires 50,000 bags of cement for the year. It costs $6.25 to place an order and $10 annually to carry a unit in inventory. The economic order quantity in units is:
   a. 2,500
   c. 250
   b. 500
   d. 5,000

6. The expected daily usage of an item of material is 175 units, the anticipated lead time is 8 days and the required safety stock is 1,000 units. The order point is:
   a. 2,400
   c. 675
   b. 1,170
   d. 1,000

7. A relevant factor in determining economic order quantity is:
   a. Physical plant insurance costs
   b. Warehouse supervisory salaries
   c. Variable costs of processing a purchase order
   d. Physical plant depreciation charges

8. When defective work occurs on orders that the company regularly produces, the additional costs of correcting the imperfections are charged to:
   a. Extraordinary losses
   b. The specific job in which the spoilage occurred
   c. Administrative expenses
   d. Factory overhead control

9. If Felix Company orders raw materials in quantities smaller than the optimum quantity obtained using the basic EOQ model, in order to obtain a quantity discount, the company will experience:
   a. Ordering costs higher than if the optimum quantity were ordered
   b. Ordering costs the same as if the optimum quantity were ordered
   c. Carrying costs higher than ordering costs
   d. Ordering costs the same as carrying costs

10. Ignoring safety stocks, a valid computation of the order point is:
    a. The economic order quantity
    b. The economic order quantity multiplied by the anticipated demand during the lead time
    c. The anticipated demand during the lead time
    d. The square root of the anticipated demand during the lead time

Part IV

Martinez Co. has the following data available relative to its investment in materials:

Number of units of material used annually	20,000
Number of workdays in a year......................................	250
Cost of placing an order...	$20
Annual carrying cost per unit of inventory....................	$5

Instructions:

1. Compute the economic order quantity.

2. Using the above data, compute the order size that results in the minimum total order and carrying cost by completing the following table.

(1) Order Size	(2) Number of Orders	(3) Total Order Cost	(4) Average Inventory	(5) Total Carrying Cost	(6) Total Order & Carrying Costs
100					
200					
300					
400					
500					
600					
700					
800					

3. If the company requires a safety stock of 200 units and has an anticipated lead time of 5 days, what is the order point?

Part V

Custom Ceramics Inc. makes the following purchases and issues of a new material during March:

March	2	Received 200 lbs. @ $9; total cost, $1,800.
	8	Received 60 lbs. @ $10; total cost, $600.
	18	Issued 100 lbs.
	24	Received 240 lbs. @ $12; total cost, $2,880.
	31	Issued 200 lbs.

Instructions: Using a perpetual inventory system and the materials ledger cards provided, state the cost of materials consumed and the cost assigned to the inventory at the end of March.

1. First-in, first-out costing

Date	Received			Issued			Balance		
	Quantity	Unit Price	Amount	Quantity	Unit Price	Amount	Quantity	Unit Price	Amount

Cost of materials consumed .... $_____

Cost assigned to inventory .... $_____

2. Last-in, first-out costing

Date	Received			Issued			Balance		
	Quantity	Unit Price	Amount	Quantity	Unit Price	Amount	Quantity	Unit Price	Amount

Cost of materials consumed...................... $_____

Cost assigned to inventory .... $_____

3. Moving average method (Round to the nearest cent)

Date	Received			Issued			Balance		
	Quantity	Unit Price	Amount	Quantity	Unit Price	Amount	Quantity	Unit Price	Amount

Cost of materials consumed...................... $_____

Cost assigned to inventory .... $_____

Part VI

The following accounts are maintained by the Fielding Fabricators Inc. in its general ledger: Materials, Work in Process, Factory Overhead, Accounts Payable, and Cash. The materials account had a debit balance of $75,000 and the cash account had a debit balance of $100,000 on September 1. A summary of materials transactions for September shows:

a. Materials purchased on account, $125,500
b. Direct materials issued, $90,900
c. Direct materials returned to storeroom, $3,750
d. Indirect materials issued, $4,850
e. Indirect materials returned to storeroom, $720
f. Payment of invoices, $98,250
g. Materials on hand at the end of the month were less than the store's ledger balance by $250.

Instructions:

1. Prepare general journal entries in the form provided to record the materials transactions.

No.	Account	Debit	Credit

Name _____

2. Enter any beginning balances and post the general journal entries to the T-accounts provided below.

| Cash | Materials | Work in Process |

| Accounts Payable | Factory Overhead |

3. The balance of the materials account on September 30 is $_____ .

Part VII

<u>Instructions:</u> Prepare journal entries for each of the following situations:

1. The entry to record the cash sale of scrap with a minimal value of $200 that was identified as produced by Job AC101. (The company treats income from scrap as a reduction in manufacturing costs.)

Account	Debit	Credit

2. The revenue from the sale of scrap is expected to be significant ($2,000), and management wants to spread scrap revenues over the cost of all jobs produced during the period.

a. The entry to record the transfer of scrap to inventory:

Account	Debit	Credit

b. The entry to record the sale of scrap, on account, for the $2,000 estimated:

Account	Debit	Credit

3. Job Order AC102, which cost $25 per unit to produce, resulted in 10 irregular units that have a market value of $15 each. Prepare the journal entry to record the estimated market value of the irregular units if the cost of spoilage is to be charged to the specific job on which the spoilage occurred.

Account	Debit	Credit

4. The cost of correcting defective work on Job AC103 is $300 for materials, $200 for labor, and $100 for factory overhead. Prepare the journal entry to record the costs to correct the defective work if the additional cost is to be charged to all jobs worked on during the period.

Account	Debit	Credit

Part VIII (Appendix)

Jefferson-Clinton Inc., which uses backflush costing, had the following transactions during the month of May:

a. Purchased raw materials on account, $160,000.
b. Requisitioned raw materials to production, $80,000.
c. Distributed direct labor costs, $20,000.
d. Manufacturing overhead incurred, $120,000. (Use Various Credits for the account in the credit part of the entry.)
e. Completed and sold all units produced.

Instructions: Prepare general journal entries in the form provided to record the above transactions, assuming that the trigger points are the purchase of materials and the sale of finished goods.

Account	Debit	Credit

CHAPTER 3 ACCOUNTING FOR LABOR

Review Summary

1. **Direct labor** is the portion of payroll cost allocated directly to the product by a debit to the work in process account. **Indirect labor** consists of all other labor used in the manufacturing process and is charged to the factory overhead account. Accounting for labor involves: recording the time worked and/or the quantity of output by the employee; analyzing employees' time to determine how well it was utilized; allocating the factory labor costs to the proper accounts; and preparing the payroll.

2. Under an **hourly-rate wage plan** the employee's wages are computed by multiplying the established hourly rate times the hours worked. Although widely used and easy to apply, it doesn't provide any incentive to achieve a high level of productivity. Under a **piece-rate plan**, earnings are based on a worker's quantity of production. Such a plan provides an incentive for the worker to produce a high level of output, but it may encourage sacrificing quality for quantity, and it also requires more record keeping and updating of piece rates. A **modified wage plan** may set a minimum wage that will be paid even if an established quota is not met, while an additional payment for each piece beyond the established quota is added to the minimum rate.

3. The **timekeeping department** is responsible for determining the number of labor hours that the company should pay for and the type of work that the employees performed. Timekeeping maintains the clock cards, time tickets, and production reports. **Clock cards** are used to account for the total amount of time employees spend in the plant. **Time tickets** are used to record the hours that an employee works on individual jobs. **Individual production reports** show the total number of units completed, by job, and are used in place of time tickets when a piece-rate system is used. The **payroll department** is responsible for computing employee gross earnings, deductions, and net pay. The payroll department maintains payroll records, employee earnings records, and payroll summaries. A **payroll record** provides information on each employee for one pay period relative to marital status, withholding allowances, pay rate, hours worked per day, regular and overtime earnings, deductions, and net pay. The **employee earnings record** is a record of the earnings for a single employee for the accounting period and includes information on pay rates, regular and overtime hours worked, total earnings, withholdings, deductions, and net pay.

4. The **labor cost summary** form is prepared from the employee time tickets or individual production reports, and it is used for the preparation of a general journal entry that distributes the payroll to the proper accounts. Work in Process is debited for the regular-time wages of direct labor, Factory Overhead is debited for indirect wages and usually for overtime premium, and Payroll is credited for the total. If the overtime work on a particular job resulted from random scheduling, then the overtime premium should be charged to Factory Overhead and spread over all jobs; whereas if the overtime resulted from the unique demands of a specific job, then the overtime premium should be charged to Work in Process and the particular job that caused its incurrence.

5. **Payroll taxes** imposed on employers include social security tax and federal and state unemployment taxes. The **Federal Insurance Contribution Act (FICA)** requires employers to pay social security tax on wages and salaries equal to the amount of tax withheld from employee's earnings. The Federal Unemployment Tax Act (FUTA) requires employers to pay an **established** rate of tax on wages and salaries to provide for compensation to employees laid off from their jobs. Employers' contributions are apportioned between the federal government, which administers the unemployment compensation program, and the state governments, which actually pay out the benefits. Since payroll tax rates and wage bases frequently change, this text assumes an 8% tax rate on the first $70,000 of FICA wages, and a 4% rate for state taxes and a 1% rate for federal taxes on the first $8,000 of wages for unemployment compensation.

6. **Shift premiums** are paid to employees who do not work the regular day shift. Because these premiums are paid for inconvenient hours rather than increased productivity, they should be charged to Factory Overhead rather than to Work in Process to avoid distorting the cost of certain jobs. **Defined benefit pension plans** determine benefits based on an employee's level of income and length of service. **Defined contribution pension plans** specify the maximum contribution that can be made to an employee's account during the year, but the amount of pension benefits is based on the performance of the investment vehicles that the employee selected. **Non-contributory plans** are completely funded by the company, whereas **contributory plans** require a partial contribution from the employee. The company should accrue, systematically, the total estimated pension cost from the date the plan started to the date the employee retires. Current pension costs for factory employees are part of the cost of production and may be charged to Factory Overhead, or they may be charged to General Administrative Expense under the premise that the costs of pensions are beneficial to the company as a whole. Bonus pay, vacation pay, and holiday pay are considered to be earned gradually during the employee's time on the job, and therefore a portion of this liability is accrued each payroll period that the employee is on the job.

Part I

Instructions: Indicate your answer in the Answers column by writing a "T" for True or an "F" for False.

Answers

1. The cost of direct labor is charged to the factory overhead account......... _____

2. A serious limitation of an hourly-rate wage plan is that no incentive is provided by the plan design to maintain a high degree of employee productivity. .... _____

3. Incentive-wage plans are often introduced by management over the objection of labor unions.. _____

4. Timekeeping and Payroll should function as independent units to serve as an internal check on the accuracy of each other's work. .... _____

5. Individual production reports are used in place of time tickets when a company uses a piece-rate wage plan.. _____

6. The payroll record contains the earnings history for a single employee, whereas the employee earnings record shows the earnings data for all employees for a specific payroll period.. _____

7. The debit posted to Factory Overhead for payroll costs must equal the indirect labor cost recorded in the factory overhead ledger. .... _____

8. If the overtime hours incurred on a job were merely the result of random scheduling, the cost of the overtime premium should be charged to the specific job worked on during the overtime period.. _____

9. Employers and employees share equally the cost of the social security program.. _____

10. In theory, payroll taxes on factory direct labor should be charged to Work in Process as direct labor, but in practice they usually are included in Factory Overhead. .... _____

11. The unemployment insurance program is administered by the individual states, but claims payments are made by the federal government. .... _____

12. Shift premiums usually are charged to Factory Overhead in order to avoid a substantial distortion of worker productivity. .... _____

13. In highly-automated manufacturing settings, direct labor cost is usually the most significant production cost. .... _____

14. Defined contribution pension plans specify the exact amount of retirement income that an employee will receive. .... _____

15. The costs of vacation pay and holiday pay should be accrued in the periods that the employees actually work.. _____

Part II

Instructions: In the Answers column, place the letter from the list below that identifies the term that best matches the statement. No letter should be used more than once.

a. Payroll department
b. Payroll record
c. Defined contribution plans
d. Direct labor
e. Employee earnings record
f. Contributory plans
g. Bar codes

h. Hourly-rate plan
i. Indirect labor
j. Federal Unemployment Tax Act
k. Defined benefit plans
l. Non-contributory plans
m. Modified wage plan
n. Shift premium

o. Federal Insurance Contribution Act
p. Piece-rate plan
q. Time ticket
r. Payroll taxes
s. Bonuses, vacations, and holiday pay
t. Timekeeping department

Answers

_____ 1. This is the labor charged to the product by a debit to the work in process account.

_____ 2. This consists of all other types of labor used in the manufacturing process and is charged to the factory overhead account.

_____ 3. This is a widely accepted wage plan that is simpler to use than other plans.

_____ 4. Under this type of wage plan, earnings are based on the worker's quantity of production.

_____ 5. An example of this type of plan would be a set minimum wage plus an additional payment per piece if the established quota is exceeded.

_____ 6. The responsibilities of this department include determining the number of hours that the company should pay for the type of work the employees performed.

_____ 7. This department is assigned the responsibility of computing each employee's gross earnings, the amount of withholding, and the net pay.

_____ 8. These are pension plans whose retirement benefit payments are based on the performance of the investment vehicles chosen by the employees.

_____ 9. This becomes the source document for allocating the labor costs to jobs or departments in the cost ledger and factory overhead ledger.

_____ 10. Even though these are received at specific times during the year, their costs are accrued throughout the year.

_____ 11. This is a summary listing of employees' earnings and includes such items as marital status, number of withholding allowances, rate of pay, FICA taxable earnings, deductions, and net amount paid.

_____ 12. This is an auxiliary record for the earnings of each employee.

_____ 13. These are symbols that can be processed electronically to identify numbers, letters, or special characters.

_____ 14. These are pension plans that require a partial contribution by the employees.

_____ **15.** These are imposed on employers and include social security tax and federal and state unemployment taxes.

_____ **16.** It requires employers to pay social security taxes on wages and salaries equal to the amount withheld from employee earnings.

_____ **17.** This requires employers to pay an established rate of tax on wages and salaries to provide for compensation to employees if they should be laid off from their regular jobs.

_____ **18.** This usually is added to the regular rate of pay for employees who do not work a normal day shift.

_____ **19.** These are pension plans that specify the amount of benefits that an employee will receive based on earnings and length of service.

_____ **20.** These are pension plans that are completely funded by the company.

Part III

Instructions: In the Answers column, place the letter of the choice that most correctly completes each item.

Answers

_____ **1.** Effective internal control over the payroll function includes:
a. Reconciling total time recorded on clock cards to job reports submitted by employees responsible for those specific jobs
b. Supervising payroll department employees by personnel department management
c. Maintaining employee personnel records by payroll department employees
d. Comparing total time spent on jobs with total time indicated on clock cards

_____ **2.** The document that provides evidence of an employee's total time in the plant is the:
a. Time ticket   c. Clock card
b. Daily performance report   d. Requisition

_____ **3.** An example of a fringe cost is:
a. The direct labor wage rate
b. Withheld taxes
c. Union dues paid by the employee
d. The employer portion of FICA tax

_____ **4.** The wage plan which most bases an employee's earnings on the quantity of the employee's production is termed a(n):
a. Hourly-rate plan   c. Piece-rate plan
b. Modified wage plan   d. None of the above

_____ 5. In job order costing, payroll taxes paid by the employer for factory employees are usually accounted for as:
a. Direct labor
b. Factory overhead
c. Indirect labor
d. Administrative costs

_____ 6. When a rush order is received during the week and it must be completed during an overtime shift, the overtime premium is charged to:
a. General and Administrative Expenses
b. Accrued Overtime Premium Receivable
c. Factory Overhead Control
d. The job worked on during the overtime period

_____ 7. An employee is paid a base rate of $800 per week for 52 weeks. The employee is entitled to a four-week vacation each year. Factory Overhead Control is debited each week for accrued vacation pay of:
a. $64.00
b. $0
c. $61.54
d. $66.67

_____ 8. To spread the cost of an annual bonus over production throughout the year, the weekly payroll entry would include a debit to which of the following accounts for the bonus portion of the entry?
a. Work in Process
b. Factory Overhead Control
c. Payroll
d. Liability for Bonus

_____ 9. Due to practical considerations, all factory-related payroll taxes usually are:
a. Allocated between direct and indirect labor
b. Charged to direct labor
c. Charged to factory overhead
d. Charged to general administrative expense

_____ 10. In a highly-automated manufacturing environment, the production cost that is usually the lowest of the following costs would be:
a. Direct materials
b. Direct labor
c. Indirect labor
d. Depreciation on machinery and equipment

Part IV

R. Clemens, an employee of the Yankee Clipper Co., submitted the following data for work activities last week:

Day	Units Produced Each Day
Monday	30
Tuesday	32
Wednesday	46
Thursday	28
Friday	34

During the week, Clemens worked eight hours each day. Compensation was based on a modified wage plan where an employee earns $2.50 per finished unit and is guaranteed a minimum of $10 per hour.

Instructions: Complete the schedule below. (Round labor cost per unit to the nearest whole cent.)

Day	Earnings at $10 per Hour	Earnings at $2.50 per Piece	Make-up Guarantee	Daily Earnings	Labor Cost per Unit
Monday					
Tuesday					
Wednesday					
Thursday					
Friday					

NOTE: Unless otherwise directed, use the following rates in the remaining parts of this chapter: FICA tax, 8%; FUTA tax, 1%; state unemployment insurance tax, 4%. Assume also that the base wage amounts, beyond which taxes are not due, have not been reached.

Part V

The information below, taken from the daily time tickets of Bengal Tiger Manufacturing Inc., summarizes time and piecework for the week ended January 30.

Employee	Clock No.	Job No.	Hours Worked	Production Pieces	Hourly Rate	Piece Rate
Dillon, C..............	37	347	40	780	–	$.50
Smith, A.	38	–	40	–	$ 7.00	–
Spikes, T.............	39	343	46	–	8.80	–
Warrick, P.	40	–	40	–	12.20	–

The company operates on a 40-hour week and pays time and a half for overtime. FICA tax deductions should be made for each employee. A 3% deduction is to be made from each employee's wage for health insurance. Smith works as a forklift operator; Warrick is the supervisor; the others work directly on the jobs. Use 15% in computing income tax withheld.

Instructions:

1. Using the form provided below, determine each employee's gross pay, deductions, and net pay.

	Dillon	Smith	Spikes	Warrick	Total
Hours worked.................					
Piecework......................					
Rate (hourly/piece)					
Direct labor					
Indirect labor.................					
Overtime premium.........					
Gross pay......................	$	$	$	$	$
Income tax (15%)..........	$	$	$	$	$
FICA tax (8%)...............					
Health insurance (3%) ...					
Total deductions.............					
Net pay	$	$	$	$	$

2. Prepare journal entries to (a) set up the accrued payroll and other liabilities, (b) pay the payroll, (c) distribute the payroll, and (d) record the employer's payroll taxes.

Account	Debit	Credit
(a)		
(b)		
(c)		
(d)		

Part VI

An employee of the Molding Department is paid $20 per hour for a regular week of 40 hours. During the week ended March 15, the employee worked 50 hours and earned time and a half for the overtime hours.

Instructions:

1. Prepare the entry to distribute the labor cost if the job worked on during overtime was a rush order, the contract price of which included the overtime premium.

Account	Debit	Credit

2. Prepare the entry to distribute the labor cost if the job worked on during overtime was the result of random scheduling.

Account	Debit	Credit

Part VII

A production worker earns $2,200 per month and the company pays the worker a year-end bonus equal to one month's wages. The worker receives a one-month paid vacation per year and 10 paid holidays per year. Bonus, vacation benefits, and holiday pay are treated as indirect costs and accrued during the 11 months that the employee is at work.

Instructions: Prepare the journal entry to distribute the payroll and the costs and liabilities associated with the bonus, vacation pay, and holiday pay of the production worker for a month.

Account	Debit	Credit

CHAPTER 4 ACCOUNTING FOR FACTORY OVERHEAD

Review Summary

1. **Variable overhead costs,** such as power and supplies, move in direct proportion to changes in production. **Fixed overhead costs,** such as property taxes, insurance, and straight-line depreciation, remain unchanged as production levels change. **Semi-variable overhead costs** either change as certain levels of production are reached, Type A (for example, factory supervision), or they vary continuously but not in direct proportion to volume changes, Type B (for example, maintenance costs).

2. The methods used for isolating the fixed and variable elements of a semivariable expense include (1) the observation method, (2) the high-low method, and (3) the scattergraph method. With the **observation method,** the relationship of the change in expense to the change in production is examined by observation, and a decision is made to either treat the semivariable expense as a variable item or a fixed item, depending upon which it more closely resembles. The **high-low method** compares a high volume and its related cost to a low volume and its related cost, and thus determines the variable amount per unit and the fixed element of the semivariable cost. The **scattergraph** method estimates a straight line along which the semivariable costs will fall. The point where the straight line intersects the y-axis represents total fixed costs. The variable cost per unit is computed by subtracting fixed costs from total costs at any point on the graph and then dividing by the volume level for that point. The isolation of fixed and variable cost components using one of the above methods permits the preparation of a **flexible budget** that shows the expected factory overhead at any anticipated level of production.

3. In a small manufacturing company having one production department, all the factory overhead accounts may be kept in the general ledger. When the factory overhead accounts are numerous, a factory overhead subsidiary ledger, known as the **factory overhead ledger**, is kept and the control account in the general ledger is Factory Overhead. Individual accounts in the factory overhead ledger should be given titles that are clearly descriptive of the nature of the expense. In addition to the expenses that are related to the operation of the factory and the manufacturing process, factory overhead includes the cost of factory employee fringe benefits.

4. In a departmentalized manufacturing company, each factory overhead expense should be analyzed carefully to determine the kind and amount of expense to charge to each department. In a moderately sized company, the factory overhead ledger can be expanded to include a separate account for each department's share of each kind of expense. In larger companies, **factory overhead analysis sheets** are used to keep a subsidiary record of factory overhead expenses. An **expense-type analysis sheet** system has a separate sheet for each type of expense that contains ruled amount columns for each department. A **department-type analysis sheet** system has a separate sheet for each department, with each sheet containing separate ruled amount columns for each type of expense.

5. A **production department**, such as machining or assembly, is one in which actual manufacturing operations are performed, and the materials being processed are physically changed. A **service department,** such as building maintenance or the power plant, does not work on the product but rather services the needs of the production departments. Total product costs should therefore include a share of service department costs. The cost of operating each service department should be distributed to the production departments in proportion to the benefit that each service department renders to each production department. The type of work done by each service department should be determined and a base, such as floor space or number of workers, should be selected that equitably allocates the service department cost to the production departments.

6. Methods used for distributing service department costs to production departments include (1) distributing service department costs directly to production departments only (**direct distribution method**); (2) distributing service department costs sequentially to other service departments and to production departments (**step-down method**); or (3) distributing service department costs to other service departments and to production departments using algebraic methods (**algebraic distribution method**). When service department costs are allocated to producing departments only, the results may be more easily attained but are less accurate than the allocations obtained using the other methods. The rule to follow under method (2) is to distribute first the costs of the service department that services the greatest number of departments. If such a determination cannot readily be made, the department with the largest total overhead should be allocated first.

7. Since management needs to know the cost of a job or process soon after its completion, the job must be charged with an estimated amount of overhead upon completion rather than at the end of the period when the actual overhead is known. The **predetermined factory overhead rate** is determined by dividing the budgeted factory overhead by the budgeted production for the period. Budgeted production usually is expressed in terms of direct labor costs, direct labor hours, or machine hours. In a departmentalized company, a separate factory overhead rate should be used for each production department.

8. The most popular methods of applying factory overhead to jobs or processes are (1) the direct labor cost method, (2) the direct labor hour method, (3) the machine hour method, and (4) the activity-based costing method. The **direct labor cost method** uses the amount of direct labor cost that has been charged to the product as the basis for applying factory overhead. The **direct labor hour method** overcomes the problem of varying wage rates inherent in the direct labor cost method by using only the number of direct labor hours spent on the job as the basis for applying overhead. The **machine hour method** uses the number of machine hours that have been worked on the job or process as the basis for applying factory overhead. **Activity-based costing (ABC)** considers non-volume related activities that create overhead costs, such as the number of machine setups or product design changes, as well as volume-related activities, such as machine hours or direct labor hours. It is important to select the method that allocates the estimated factory overhead in the same amounts as the actual factory overhead expenses are incurred.

9. The estimated factory overhead is applied to production by a debit to Work in Process and a credit to Applied Factory Overhead. At the end of the period, the applied factory overhead account is closed to the factory overhead control account. If the factory overhead control account has a debit balance after the applied factory overhead is closed to it, that means the actual factory overhead (debits) was greater than applied factory overhead (credits) and overhead is said to be **underapplied**. A credit balance in Factory Overhead indicates that more overhead was applied than was actually incurred and overhead is said to be **overapplied**. If the year-end balance in Under- and Overapplied Factory Overhead will not materially change net income, it is closed to Cost of Goods Sold; whereas if it will materially alter net income, it should be prorated to Work in Process, Finished Goods, and Cost of Goods Sold.

Part I

Instructions: Indicate your answer in the Answers column by writing a "T" for True or an "F" for False.

Answers

1. Factory overhead includes indirect materials, indirect labor, and all other indirect manufacturing expenses. ....

2. Examples of variable factory overhead costs include property taxes and insurance on factory equipment. ....

3. Examples of Type B semivariable factory overhead costs include inspection and handling, and factory supervision. ....

4. The scattergraph method estimates the straight line along which semivariable costs will fall. ....

5. The high-low method presents a solution that has been calculated with a high degree of mathematical precision. ....

6. A flexible budget shows the expected factory overhead at any level of production. ....

7. An expense-type analysis sheet system provides a separate sheet for each type of factory overhead expense incurred. ....

8. Total product costs should include a share of service department costs as well as the costs of production departments. ....

9. The rule to follow in distributing service department costs is to first distribute the costs of the service department that services the greatest number of other departments. ....

10. The sequential distribution method is the simplest method of distributing service department costs. ....

11. Predetermined factory overhead rates are not very popular in practice because it is not important to know the cost of a job or process until the end of the period. ....

12. Varying wage rates are more of a problem when using the direct labor cost method of applying overhead than the direct labor hour method. ....

13. A credit balance in Factory Overhead, after Applied Factory Overhead has been closed, indicates that more overhead was applied than actually was incurred. ....

14. When the year-end balance in Under- and Overapplied Factory Overhead is large, it should be closed to Work in Process, Finished Goods, and Cost of Goods Sold so as not to distort net income for the period. ....

15. The entry to close Applied Factory Overhead to Factory Overhead Control is a debit to Factory Overhead Control and a credit to Applied Factory Overhead. ....

Name _____

Part II

Instructions: In the Answers column, place the letter from the list below that identifies the term that best matches the statement. No letter should be used more than once.

a. Direct distribution method
b. Flexible budget
c. Service department
d. Departmental-type analysis sheet
e. Expense-type analysis sheet
f. Variable factory overhead
g. Scattergraph method

h. High-low method
i. Type B semi-variable overhead costs
j. Sequential distribution method
k. Activity-based costing
l. Cost driver
m. Direct labor hour method
n. Machine hour method

o. Factory overhead ledger
p. Predetermined factory overhead rate
q. Applied Factory Overhead
r. Production department
s. Type A semivariable overhead costs
t. Factory Overhead

Answers

_____ 1. These factory costs can be readily forecast because they move up or down proportionately to production changes.

_____ 2. These factory costs will remain constant over a range of production and then abruptly change.

_____ 3. In this method of identifying the fixed and variable elements of a semivariable expense, the difference in volume between two points is compared to the difference in costs.

_____ 4. In activity-based costing, it is the basis used to allocate each of the activity cost pools.

_____ 5. In this method of analyzing cost behavior, the observation of cost and production data are plotted on graph paper and only intuitive judgment is used to draw a regression line.

_____ 6. This shows the expected factory overhead at any level of production.

_____ 7. Individual accounts representing various indirect manufacturing expenses are kept in this.

_____ 8. The actual overhead costs incurred during the period are charged to this account.

_____ 9. This form provides a separate amount column for each department, making it possible to distribute expenses on a departmental basis as they are recorded.

_____ 10. This form provides a separate amount column for each kind of expense incurred, making it possible to distribute the expenses on a departmental basis as they are recorded.

_____ 11. This method distributes service department costs only to production departments.

_____ 12. These are essential to the functioning of the organization but do not work on the product.

_____ 13. This is where actual manufacturing operations are performed and the units being processed are physically changed.

_____ 14. This is computed by dividing the budgeted factory overhead by the budgeted production for the period.

_____ 15. An advantage of this method of applying factory overhead is that the amount of factory overhead applied to a job is not affected by the mix of labor rates.

_____ 16. This method of applying factory overhead is most useful when the greater part of a department's production is automated.

_____ 17. These factory costs will vary continuously, but not in direct proportion to volume changes.

_____ 18. The estimated factory overhead is applied to production by a credit to this account.

_____ 19. It considers non-volume-related activities that create overhead costs as well as volume-related activities.

_____ 20. This method distributes service department costs regressively to other service departments and to production departments.

Part III

Instructions: In the Answers column, place the letter of the choice that most correctly completes each item.

Answers

_____ 1. Overapplied factory overhead always will result when a predetermined factory overhead rate is employed and:
a. Production is greater than defined capacity
b. Actual overhead costs are more than expected
c. Defined capacity is less than normal capacity
d. Overhead incurred is less than applied overhead

_____ 2. If a predetermined factory overhead rate is not used and the volume of production is decreased from the level planned, the cost per unit would be expected to:
a. Remain unchanged for fixed cost and increase for variable cost
b. Increase for fixed cost and remain unchanged for variable cost
c. Increase for fixed cost and decrease for variable cost
d. Decrease for fixed cost and remain unchanged for variable cost

_____ 3. Factory overhead should be allocated on the basis of:
   a. An activity basis that relates to cost incurrence
   b. Direct labor hours
   c. Direct labor cost
   d. Machine hours

_____ 4. A company found that the differences in product costs resulting from the application of predetermined factory overhead rates rather than actual factory overhead rates were immaterial, even though actual production was substantially less than planned production. The most likely explanation is that:
   a. Factory overhead was composed chiefly of variable costs
   b. Several products were produced simultaneously
   c. Fixed factory overhead was a significant cost
   d. Costs of factory overhead items were substantially larger than anticipated

_____ 5. When a large manufacturing company has a highly skilled labor force with varying wage rates producing different products, the most appropriate base for applying factory overhead to work in process is:
   a. Direct labor hours   c. Machine hours
   b. Direct labor dollars   d. Cost of materials used

_____ 6. The overhead application method that considers non-volume-related activities that create overhead costs as well as volume-related activities is:
   a. Direct labor hours   c. Machine hours
   b. Direct labor dollars   d. Activity-based costing

_____ 7. A segment of an organization is referred to as a service department if it has:
   a. Responsibility for developing markets for and selling of the organization's output
   b. Responsibility for combining the raw materials, direct labor, and other production factors into a final output
   c. Authority to make decisions affecting the major determinants of profit, including the power to choose its markets and sources of supply
   d. Authority to provide specialized support to other units within the organization

_____ 8. A department that would be classified as a service department is:
   a. Assembly   c. Forming
   b. Human Resources   d. Finishing

_____ 9. The most reasonable base for allocating the cost of a human resources department is:
   a. Number of employees   c. Square footage
   b. Materials used   d. Building depreciation

_____ 10. The method for allocating service department costs that results in the least precision is:
   a. Direct method   c. Algebraic method
   b. Sequential method   d. Step-down method

Part IV

The O'Reilly Company has accumulated the following data over a six-month period:

	Direct Labor Hours	Electricity Expense Supervision
July	460	$ 25,000
August	620	30,000
September	580	28,000
October	680	35,000
November	320	22,000
December	720	38,000
	3,380	$178,000

Instructions: Separate the supervision expense into its fixed and variable components using the high-low method.

	Direct Labor Hours	Electricity Expense
High volume	_____	_____
Low volume	_____	_____
Difference	_____	_____

Variable cost per direct labor hour:

Total fixed cost:

Part V

Chaucer Chemical Co. consists of three production departments and four service departments. For the purpose of creating factory overhead rates, the accountant prepared the cost distribution sheet, shown on the next page, containing collected operational data. For the distribution of expenses of the service departments, the following procedures and order of distribution had been decided upon:

a. Utilities: 70% on metered hours—power; 30% on floor square footage

b. Maintenance: Maintenance hours excluding Utilities

c. Materials Handling: 45% to Preparation; 35% to Mixing; and 20% to Packaging

d. Factory Office: Preparation, 50%; Mixing, 40%; Packaging, 10%

Instructions: Complete the cost distribution sheet using the sequential (step-down) method. No reciprocal charging should take place. Factory overhead rates should be based on pounds handled in Preparation and Mixing (500,000 in Preparation; 300,000 in Mixing) and on direct labor cost of $10,000 in Packaging. (Round all amounts except overhead rates to the nearest dollar and round overhead rates to four decimal places.)

Name _____

	Total	Production Departments			Service Departments			
		Preparation	Mixing	Packaging	Utilities	Maintenance	Materials Handling	Factory Office
Operational data:								
Floor space—sq. ft.	53,000	18,000	13,000	12,000	3,000	2,000	1,000	4,000
Maintenance hours .	7,000	3,000	1,500	600	1,000	—	600	300
Metered hours.........	5,000	1,500	1,800	700	—	500	300	200
Expenses:								
Indirect labor	$26,000	$4,500	$4,000	$3,500	$6,000	$3,500	$2,500	$2,000
Payroll taxes	2,500	450	400	350	500	350	250	200
Indirect materials....	6,000	900	1,100	3,000	500	200	50	250
Depreciation	1,000	150	200	100	200	150	75	125
Total	$35,500	$6,000	$5,700	$6,950	$7,200	$4,200	$2,875	$2,575
Distribution of service departments:								
Utilities:								
70% metered hours.								
30% sq. footage					$	$		
Maintenance						$		
							$	$
Materials handling..							$	
Factory office..........								$
	$	$	$	$				
Bases:								
Pounds handled								
Direct labor costs....								
Rates								

Part VI

Job H202 requires $5,000 of direct materials, $2,000 of direct labor, 400 direct labor hours, 200 machine hours, two setups, and one design change. The cost pools and overhead rates in each pool follow:

Cost Pool	Overhead Rate
Direct labor usage	$20/direct labor hour
Machine usage	$40/machine hour
Machine setups	$1,000/setup
Design changes	$2,000/design change

Instructions: Determine the cost of Job H202.

CHAPTER 5 PROCESS COST ACCOUNTING— GENERAL PROCEDURES

Review Summary

1. **Process costing** is used when goods of a similar nature are manufactured in a continuous production operation. Costs are accumulated by department and divided by units produced to obtain the departmental average cost per unit. In a process cost system, materials and labor costs are charged to the departments in which they are incurred. Indirect materials and indirect labor that cannot be identified with a specific department are charged to Factory Overhead. Actual overhead costs are collected in a control account in the general ledger that is supported by a subsidiary ledger consisting of **factory overhead analysis sheets** showing the detailed allocation of costs to the various departments. Predetermined overhead rates are used in process costing to apply factory overhead to departments.

2. The primary problem in process costing is the allocation of production costs between the units finished during the period and the units still in process at the end of the period. Under the **average cost method** of assigning costs to inventories, the cost of the work in process at the beginning of the period is added to the production costs for the current period, and the total is divided by the equivalent production to determine the average unit cost. **Equivalent production** is the number of whole units that could have been completed given the production costs incurred. To determine equivalent units using the average cost method, the stage of completion of units in process at the end of the period must be ascertained. Equivalent units for a period may be computed as follows under the average cost method:

$$\text{Units completed this period} + \left(\text{Units in ending work in process inventory} \times \text{\% of completion this period} \right)$$

3. Once the equivalent units of production are determined, they can be divided into the total production costs for the period to obtain the average cost per unit. The inventory costs can then be allocated between Work in Process and Finished Goods as follows:

$$\text{Cost of finished goods} = \text{Units transferred to finished goods} \times \text{Average cost per unit}$$

$$\text{Cost of work in process} = \text{Number of units in ending work in process} \times \text{\% of completion} \times \text{Average cost per unit}$$

When production costs are not incurred evenly throughout the production process, the amount of materials, labor, and overhead have to be evaluated separately in estimating the stage of completion.

4. A **cost of production summary** accumulates the materials, labor, and factory overhead costs for which a department is accountable. It contains the calculation of equivalent production for the period that consists of the units finished during the month plus the equivalent units of work in process. It also includes the computations for the unit costs for material, labor, and factory overhead that are obtained by dividing the equivalent production into the respective production costs for each element. Lastly, it summarizes

the disposition of the production costs to either the cost of goods finished during the period or the cost of work in process at the end of the period. The total costs to be accounted for during the period must equal the total production costs accounted for during the period.

5. A **production report** submitted by the departmental supervisor to the cost accountant lists the number of units in process at the beginning of the month, the number of units finished during the month, the number of units in process at the end of the month, and the estimated stage of completion of the ending work-in-process inventory. After receiving the production report, the cost accountant prepares the cost of production summary by first collecting the period's production costs from summaries of materials requisitions, payroll, and factory overhead analysis sheets. The units in process are then converted to equivalent units. The cost of production summary can be completed with the computation of the unit costs and the ending inventory costs. After preparing the cost of production summary, the accountant can debit Finished Goods and credit Work in Process for the cost of the goods finished during the period; and the statement of cost of goods manufactured can be prepared.

6. If there is beginning work-in-process inventory, the accountant considers not only the current month's cost of material, labor, and factory overhead in determining the unit costs for the month but also the cost of each element carried over from the prior month. When there are two departments, the costs accumulated in the first department for those units completed and transferred are transferred to the next department. Although still in process, the transferred units and their related costs are treated as completed production in the first department and as raw materials added at the beginning of the process in the second department. The calculation of unit cost for the month in the second department considers only those costs incurred in that department and the equivalent units produced in the department. The **transferred-in costs** and units from the first department are not included in the computation. In determining the cost transferred to finished goods and the cost of the work in process, however, the prior department costs must be considered.

7. If finished goods have been completed in a department but not yet transferred at the end of the month, they are accounted for as "goods completed and on hand" and priced out at the full unit price. For financial statement purposes, the goods still are considered to be work in process because they are complete as to the department but not as to the factory. Often the cost from prior departments will change from one month to the next, and these costs will have to be averaged on a subsequent department's cost of production summary for the purpose of assigning total costs.

Part I

Instructions: Indicate your answer in the Answers column by writing a "T" for True or an "F" for False.

Answers

1. Process costing is appropriate when goods are manufactured in a continuous or mass production operation.. _____

2. The focal point of process costing is the job. .... _____

3. The main difference between job order and process costing is the manner in which costs are accumulated. .... _____

4. A process cost system requires more clerical effort than a job order cost system because costs are charged to departments rather than to individual jobs.. _____

5. In a process cost system, overhead is applied on the basis of departments rather than jobs. .... _____

6. To compute average unit cost, the cost of the work in process at the beginning of the period is added to the production costs for the period, and the total is divided by the number of units finished. .... _____

7. The calculation of equivalent production under the average cost method requires the restatement of goods in process at the end of the period in terms of completed units. .... _____

8. The estimate of the stage of completion of work in process usually is made by an engineer... _____

9. In computing equivalent production, the number of units in ending work in process is multiplied by the percentage of their completion and then added to the units finished this period. .... _____

10. A cost of production summary presents the necessary information for inventory valuation and serves as the source for summary journal entries. .... _____

11. The factory supervisor prepares the cost of production summary by first collecting the period's production costs from summaries of material requisitions, payroll, and factory overhead analysis sheets...................... _____

12. When the cost of production summary is completed, the total costs to be accounted for should be equal to the total production costs accounted for. .... _____

13. In computing unit cost for the month when there is beginning inventory, the cost of the beginning inventory is added to the monthly production costs before dividing by equivalent production...................................... _____

14. In computing the unit cost of production in a department subsequent to the first, the transferred-in costs and units from the prior department are included in the computation... _____

15. If at the end of the period, goods are completed and on hand in the first department of a production process that requires two departments, they would be included as finished goods for financial statement purposes.... _____

Part II

Instructions: In the Answers column, place the letter from the list below that identifies the term that best matches the statement. No letter should be used more than once.

a. Average cost method
b. Production report
c. Cost center
d. Work in process
e. Equivalent production

f. Cost of production summary
g. Process cost system
h. Transferred-in cost
i. Stage of completion
j. Job order cost system

Answers

_____ 1. This cost system is appropriate when products are manufactured on a special order basis.

_____ 2. A unit of activity within the factory to which costs may be assigned practically and equitably.

_____ 3. Under this method of process costing, the cost of the beginning work in process is added to the production cost for the current period in the unit cost calculation.

_____ 4. The number of units that could have been completed during a period using the production costs incurred during the period.

_____ 5. Represents the fraction or percentage of materials, labor, and overhead costs of a completed unit that has been applied during the period to goods that have not been completed.

_____ 6. Submitted by the department head indicating the number of units in process at the beginning of the period, the number of units completed during the period, and the number of units in process at the end of the period and their stage of completion.

_____ 7. The cost of units received from a prior department.

_____ 8. This cost system is appropriate when goods of a similar or homogeneous nature are manufactured in a continuous or mass production operation.

_____ 9. Presents the necessary information for inventory valuation and can also serve as the source for summary journal entries.

_____ 10. This is what units finished but still on hand in a department at the end of the period are considered for financial statement purposes.

Part III

Instructions: In the Answers column, place the letter of the choice that most correctly completes each item.

Answers

_____ 1. For a process cost system, procedures must be designed to:
   a. Value inventory of work still in process
   b. Determine a unit cost for each department
   c. Accumulate materials, labor, and factory overhead costs by departments
   d. All of the above

_____ 2. A cost of production report for a department shows all of the following except:
   a. Total and unit costs transferred from a preceding department
   b. The cost per job
   c. Unit costs added by the department
   d. Costs transferred to a successor department or to finished goods

_____ 3. The beginning work-in-process inventory was 40 percent complete and the ending work-in-process inventory was 60 percent complete. The dollar amount of the production cost included in the ending work-in-process inventory (using the average cost method) is determined by multiplying the average unit costs by what percentage of the total units in the ending work-in-process inventory?
   a. 100 percent
   b. 60 percent
   c. 50 percent
   d. 40 percent

_____ 4. An error was made in the computation of the percentage-of-completion of the current year's ending work-in-process inventory. The error resulted in assigning a higher percentage-of-completion to each component of the inventory than actually was the case. What is the resultant effect of this error upon:
   1. The computation of equivalent units in total?
   2. The computation of costs per equivalent unit?
   3. Costs assigned to cost of goods completed for the period?

	1	**2**	**3**
a.	Understate	overstate	overstate
b.	Understate	understate	overstate
c.	Overstate	understate	understate
d.	Overstate	overstate	understate

_____ 5. Hallstead Company had 10,000 units in work in process at January 1 that were 40 percent complete. During January, 30,000 units were completed. At January 31, 12,000 units remained in work in process and were 60 percent complete. Using the average cost method, the equivalent units for January were:
   a. 28,000
   b. 34,800
   c. 37,200
   d. 26,800

_____ 6. Using the data given for (5) above, determine how many units were started during January:
   a. 20,000
   b. 28,000
   c. 42,000
   d. 32,000

7. What are the transferred-in costs as used in a process cost accounting system?
   a. Labor that is transferred from another department within the same plant instead of hiring temporary workers from the outside
   b. Costs of the product of a previous internal process that is subsequently used in a succeeding internal process
   c. Supervisory salaries that are transferred from an overhead cost center to a production cost center
   d. Ending work-in-process inventory of a previous process that will be used in a succeeding process

8. An equivalent unit of material or conversion cost is equal to:
   a. The amount of material or conversion cost necessary to complete one unit of production
   b. A unit of work-in-process inventory
   c. The amount of material or conversion cost necessary to start a unit of production in work in process
   d. Fifty percent of the material or conversion cost of a unit of finished goods inventory

9. Which of the following characteristics applies to process costing but not to job order costing?
   a. Identifiable batches of production
   b. Equivalent units of production
   c. Work-in-process inventories
   d. Use of standard costs

10. In the computation of manufacturing cost per equivalent unit, the weighted average method of process costing considers:
   a. Current costs only
   b. Current costs plus cost of beginning work-in-process inventory
   c. Current costs plus cost of ending work-in-process inventory
   d. Current costs less cost of beginning work-in-process inventory

Name _____

Part IV

From the following list of accounts, record the account(s) to be debited and credited for each of the transactions below. Assume that these transactions occur in a company that utilizes a process cost accounting system.

Accounts
Cost of Goods Sold
Factory Overhead
Factory Overhead—Department A
Factory Overhead—Department B
Finished Goods
Materials

Accounts
Payroll
Various Credits
Accounts Payable
Work in Process—Department A
Work in Process—Department B

Transaction	Debit	Credit
1. Materials and supplies purchased....................		
2. Direct materials issued to both departments and supplies issued to the factory.........................		
3. Direct and indirect labor cost incurred in both departments........		
4. Other factory costs incurred......................		
5. Factory overhead distributed to both departments		
6. Factory overhead applied to both departments		
7. Units transferred from Department A to Department B		
8. Units completed in Department B and transferred..................		
9. Units sold....................		

Part V

Salsa Manufacturing Company uses the process cost system and average costing. The following production data is for the month of June, 2001.

Production Costs

Work in process, beginning of month:

Materials	$3,000	
Labor	1,500	
Factory overhead	500	$ 5,000

Costs incurred during month:

Materials	$50,000	
Labor	30,000	
Factory overhead	20,000	100,000
Total		$105,000

Production Report

	Units
In process, beginning of month	1,000
Finished and transferred during month	18,000
In process, end of month	4,000
Stage of completion for materials, labor, and overhead (ending)	One-half
Stage of completion for materials, labor, and overhead (beginning)	One-fourth

Instructions: Complete the following cost of production summary for Salsa Manufacturing Company. Show computations in spaces provided and round unit costs to three decimal places.

Salsa Manufacturing Company
Cost of Production Summary
For the Month Ended June 30, 2001

Cost of work in process, beginning of month:

Materials .... $

Labor ....

Factory overhead ....   _____ $

Cost of production for month:

Materials .... $

Labor ....

Factory overhead ....   _____   _____

Total costs to be accounted for .... $_____

Unit output for month:

Finished during month..

Equivalent units of work in process, end of month

(_____)...............................   _____

Total equivalent production ....   _____

52

Unit cost for month:

Materials (_____)................... $

Labor (_____) ....

Factory overhead (_____).........   _____

    Total... $_____

Inventory costs:

  Cost of goods finished during month

    (_____)............................... $

  Cost of work in process, end of month:

    Materials (_____) .... $

    Labor (_____).......................

    Factory overhead (_____) ....   _____   _____

Total production costs accounted for.......................... $_____

Part VI

Falmouth Products manufactures one product in two departments on a continuous basis and uses the average method of process cost accounting. The following information was reported for the month of May, 2001.

Production Costs

	Machining		Assembly	
Work in process, beginning of month:				
Cost in Machining		–0–		$ 27,000
Materials	$ 4,000		$ 800	
Labor	3,000		400	
Factory overhead	2,000	$ 9,000	600	1,800
Cost incurred during month:				
Materials	$68,000		$44,000	
Labor	51,000		22,000	
Factory overhead	34,000	153,000	33,000	99,000
Total		$162,000		$125,560

Production Report

	Machining (Units)	Assembly (Units)
In process, beginning of month	1,000	1,000
Finished and transferred during month	5,000	4,000
In process, end of month	2,000	2,000
Stage of completion as to materials, labor, overhead	One-half	One-half

Instructions: Prepare a cost of production summary for each department for the month. Show computations in the spaces provided.

Falmouth Products
Cost of Production Summary—Machining
For the Month Ended May 31, 2001

Cost of work in process, beginning of month:

Materials .... $

Labor ....

Factory overhead .... _____ $

Cost of production for month:

Materials .... $

Labor ....

Factory overhead .... _____ _____

Total costs to be accounted for .... $_____

Unit output for month:

Finished and transferred to Assembly during month ....

Equivalent units of work in process, end of month
(_____) .... _____

Total equivalent production .... _____

Unit cost for month:

Materials (_____) .... $

Labor (_____) ....

Factory overhead (_____) .... _____

Total .... $_____

Inventory costs:

Cost of goods finished and transferred to Assembly during month
(_____) .... $

Cost of work in process, end of month:

Materials (_____) .... $

Labor (_____) ....

Factory overhead (_____) .... _____ _____

Total production costs accounted for.......................... $_____

Falmouth Products
Cost of Production Summary—Assembly
For the Month Ended May 31, 2001

Cost of work in process, beginning of month:

    Cost in Machining .... $

    Cost in Assembly:

        Materials...................................... $

        Labor...

        Factory overhead..........................   _____   _____ $

Cost of goods received from Machining during month..

Cost of production for month:

    Materials .... $

    Labor...

    Factory overhead ....   _____   _____

Total cost to be accounted for... $_____

Unit output for month:

    Finished and transferred to stockroom during month.

    Equivalent units of work in process, end of month

        (_____).....................................   _____

        Total equivalent production ....   _____

Unit cost for month:

    Materials (_____)......................... $

    Labor (_____) ....

    Factory overhead (_____).............   _____

        Total... $_____

Inventory costs:

Cost of goods finished and transferred to stockroom
    during month:

    Cost in Machining (_____)........... $

    Cost in Assembly (_____) ....   _____ $

Cost of work in process, end of month:

    Cost in Machining (_____)........... $

    Cost in Assembly:

        Materials

            (_____) .... $

        Labor

            (_____) ....

        Factory overhead

            (_____) ....   _____   _____

Total production costs accounted for.............................. $_____

CHAPTER 6 PROCESS COST ACCOUNTING—ADDITIONAL PROCEDURES

Review Summary

1. In many industries where a process cost system is used, the materials may be put into production in irregular quantities and at varying points in the processing cycle; whereas labor and factory overhead usually are incurred evenly throughout the production process. In these situations, equivalent production must be computed separately for each element of production cost, rather than using one equivalent unit figure for all cost elements. In addition, the allocation of cost for each element must be computed individually when valuing the ending inventory.

2. Many production processes are of such a nature that there is some loss of units during the process due to evaporation, shrinkage, etc. **Normal losses** are unavoidable losses that are considered a necessary cost of producing the marketable units. The cost of the lost units is spread over the remaining marketable units, thus increasing the unit cost of the completed units. Units lost under abnormal circumstances are included in the calculation of equivalent production, and unit costs are determined as if the units were lost at the end of the process. **Abnormal losses** are not inherent to the manufacturing process, nor are they expected under efficient operating conditions. However, the amount of the loss is charged to a separate expense account, Abnormal Loss of Units, rather than attaching to the inventory cost of the units transferred. If units are gained in production in a department subsequent to the first, the calculation of the adjusted unit cost is similar to that made when units are lost, except that the total cost of the original units is spread over a greater number of units, thus reducing the unit cost.

3. The **first-in, first-out** method of process costing assumes that costs of the current period are first applied to complete the beginning units in process, then to start and finish a number of units, and finally to start other units in process. FIFO costing differs from average costing only if there is beginning work-in-process inventory. Under FIFO, the unit output required to complete the beginning work in process must be included in the equivalent production calculation. For example:

$$\text{Equivalent production} = \begin{array}{c} \text{Work required to} \\ \text{complete beginning} \\ \text{work in process} \end{array} + \begin{array}{c} \text{Units started and} \\ \text{finished during} \\ \text{the month} \end{array} + \begin{array}{c} \text{Work done} \\ \text{on ending} \\ \text{work in process} \end{array}$$

4. Calculation of unit costs with the FIFO method takes into consideration only the current period data. The cost of the beginning work in process is not merged with current costs under the FIFO method as it is under the average cost method. When units are transferred to a subsequent department or to finished goods, the cost related to the starting units in process lose their identity and are merged with the costs of those units started and finished during the current period. The costs assigned to the ending work-in-process inventory are determined in the same manner under the FIFO method as under the average cost approach.

5. In comparing the FIFO and the average cost methods, the argument for FIFO is that units started within the current period are valued at the current period's costs and are not distorted by merging these costs with costs from the preceding period. However, this separate identity is typically not maintained when these units are transferred to the next department. The major advantage of the average cost method is that all units completed during the period have the same unit cost assigned to them, thus making average costing a simpler method to use.

6. Two or more products of significant value derived from a common process are known as **joint products.** The cost of materials, labor, and overhead incurred up to the point that the separate products can be identified—the **split-off point**—are known as **joint costs.** The **physical unit of measure method** allocates joint costs to the joint products on the basis of volume, weight, or size. The **relative sales value method** of allocating joint costs is based on the premise that the greatest share of joint costs should be borne by the products with the highest sales value. Some companies subtract the costs after split-off from the ultimate sales values of the individual products to arrive at an **adjusted sales value** that is used as the basis for allocating the joint costs.

7. When one or more of the products that result from a joint process have relatively little sales value, they are known as **by-products.** The most common method of accounting for by-products is to treat the estimated sales value of the by-product as a reduction in the inventory costs of the main products by debiting an inventory account, By-Products, and crediting Work in Process at the time the by-product is identified. If the by-product is subsequently sold for more or less than its estimated sales value, the difference may be credited or debited to Gain and Loss on Sales of By-Products. In instances where the sales value of the by-product is insignificant or uncertain, no entry is made for the by-product at the split-off point. When the by-product is subsequently sold, the by-product revenue is treated as either miscellaneous income, a reduction in cost of the main products sold, or a reduction in the cost of the main products manufactured.

Part I

Instructions: Indicate your answer in the Answers column by writing a "T" for True or an "F" for False.

1. When materials are added at varying stages of the production process, separate equivalent production figures must be used for materials and for labor and factory overhead. .... _____

2. The incurrence of overhead is usually so closely related to labor costs or labor hours that overhead is thought to be incurred in the same ratio as labor expense for purposes of computing equivalent units. .... _____

3. Abnormal losses are treated as product costs resulting in an increased unit cost for the marketable units. .... _____

4. Units lost under abnormal circumstances are included in the calculation of equivalent production, and unit costs are determined as if the units were lost at the end of the process. .... _____

5. Under the FIFO method, the work required to complete the beginning work in process is ignored in computing equivalent units. .... _____

6. Abnormal losses are treated as period costs and shown as a separate item of expense on the current income statement. .... _____

7. When materials are added in a department subsequent to the first department and additional units result, the adjusted unit cost will be more than the previous unit cost. .... _____

8. FIFO costing differs from average costing only if there are units in process at the start of the period. .... _____

9. Under the FIFO method, the cost of the beginning work in process has to be broken into its individual cost elements. .... _____

10. Under the FIFO method, the beginning units in process are not merged with the units started and finished during the period. .... _____

11. The argument for the average cost method is that the units started within the current period are valued at the current period's cost and are not distorted by being merged with costs from the preceding period. .... _____

12. The average cost method has the advantage that all units completed during the period have the same unit cost assigned to them. .... _____

13. If a product is to be processed further after the split-off point, an adjusted sales value should be used that takes into consideration the cost of the processing after split-off. .... _____

14. The relative sales value method of assigning joint costs assumes that the greatest share of joint costs should be assigned to the product that has the highest value. .... _____

15. If the estimated sales value of a by-product is relatively certain, no entry is made until the date of sale. .... _____

Name _____

Part II

Instructions: In the Answers column, place the letter from the list below that identifies the term that best matches the statement. No letter should be used more than once.

a. Abnormal losses
b. Adjusted sales value
c. Adjusted unit cost
d. By-products
e. FIFO costing
f. Joint costs
g. Joint products

h. Normal losses
i. Period costs
j. Physical unit of measure method
k. Product cost
l. Relative sales value method
m. Split-off point

Answers

_____ 1. These are current costs charged to expense and are not included as part of the inventory.

_____ 2. These are not inherent to the manufacturing process and are not expected under normal, efficient operating conditions.

_____ 3. This could be based on volume, weight, size, or grade and is one means of apportioning joint costs to joint products.

_____ 4. Assumes that costs of the current period are first applied to complete the beginning units in process, then to start and finish a number of units, and finally to start other units in process.

_____ 5. These represent a necessary cost of producing marketable units, are ignored in the calculation of equivalent production, and are treated as product costs.

_____ 6. That stage in the manufacturing process when separate joint and by-products become identifiable.

_____ 7. This is a joint product's sales value less its estimated manufacturing and selling costs after split-off.

_____ 8. The total cost of materials, labor, and overhead necessary to manufacture an item.

_____ 9. These are the primary objectives of a manufacturing process that produces two or more items from a common process.

_____ 10. A new cost calculated for units transferred from a prior department because some of these units have been lost or gained in production in the subsequent department.

_____ 11. These are secondary products with relatively little value produced from a common process.

_____ 12. A commonly used means of apportioning joint costs to joint products that is based on the selling price of a joint product as it relates to the total selling price of all joint products.

_____ 13. The costs of materials, labor, and overhead incurred during a manufacturing process that produces two or more products.

Part III

Instructions: In the Answers column, place the letter of the choice that most correctly completes each item.

Answers

_____ 1. In a process costing system, if units are lost at the beginning or during the process of production and the loss is normal, the determination of equivalent units should:
   a. Ignore the units lost
   b. Assign the cost of units lost to units transferred out
   c. Use all of the units lost in the computation
   d. None of the above

_____ 2. Costs should be charged against revenue in the period in which costs are incurred except:
   a. For factory overhead costs for a product manufactured and sold in the same accounting period
   b. When the costs will not benefit any future period
   c. For costs from idle manufacturing capacity resulting from an unexpected shutdown
   d. For costs of normal shrinkage and spoilage incurred for the manufacture of a product in inventory

_____ 3. Materials are added at the start of the process in Graeter Company's mixing department, the first stage of the production cycle. The following information is available for the month of July:

	Units
Work in process, July 1 (50% complete as to materials and conversion costs)	40,000
Started in July	120,000
Transferred to the next department	90,000
Lost in production	20,000
Work in process, July 31 (40% complete as to materials and conversion costs)	50,000

Under Graeter's cost accounting system, the costs incurred on the lost units are absorbed by the remaining marketable units. Using the average cost method, what are the equivalent units for the materials unit cost calculation?
   a. 140,000   c. 90,000
   b. 110,000   d. 120,000

_____ 4. The Assembly Department is in the second stage of Forrest Company's production cycle. On May 1, the beginning work in process contained 50,000 units which were 40% complete as to conversion costs. During May, 200,000 units were transferred in from the first stage of Forrest's production cycle. On May 31, the ending work in process contained 40,000 units which were 20%

complete as to conversion costs. Material costs are added at the beginning of the process. Using the average cost method, the equivalent units were:

	Materials	Conversion Costs
a.	210,000	200,000
b.	250,000	250,000
c.	250,000	218,000
d.	210,000	218,000

_____ 5. The FIFO method of process costing differs from the average method in that the FIFO method:
   a. Considers the stage of completion of beginning work-in-process inventory in computing equivalent units of production, but the average method does not
   b. Does not consider the stage of completion of beginning work-in-process inventory in computing equivalent units of production, but the average method does
   c. Is applicable only to those companies using the FIFO inventory pricing method, but the average method may be used with any inventory pricing method
   d. Allocates costs based on whole units, but the average method uses equivalent units

_____ 6. When using the FIFO process costing method, the correct equivalent units of production for use in computing unit costs is equal to the number of units:
   a. Started into process during the period, plus the number of units in work in process at the beginning of the period
   b. In work in process at the beginning of the period, plus the number of units started during the period, plus the number of units remaining in work in process at the end of the period times the percent of work necessary to complete these units
   c. In work in process at the beginning of the period times the percent of work necessary to complete the items, plus the number of units started and completed during the period, plus the number of units remaining in work in process at the end of the period times the percent of work performed on these units during the period
   d. Transferred out during the period, plus the number of units remaining in work in process at the end of the period times the percent of work necessary to complete the units

_____ 7. A condition in which the FIFO process costing method will produce the same cost of goods manufactured as the average method is:
   a. When goods produced are homogeneous in nature
   b. When there is no beginning inventory
   c. When there are no lost units
   d. When beginning and ending inventories are each fifty percent complete

8. The components of production allocable as joint costs when a single manufacturing process produces several salable products are:
   a. Materials, labor, and factory overhead
   b. Materials and labor only
   c. Labor and factory overhead only
   d. Factory overhead and materials only

9. If two or more products share a common process before they are separated, the joint costs should be allocated in a manner that:
   a. Assigns a proportionate amount of the total cost to each product by means of a quantitative basis
   b. Maximizes total earnings
   c. Minimizes variations in a unit of production cost
   d. Does not introduce an element of estimation into the process of accumulating costs for each product

10. Texas Company manufactures two products, kerosene and gasoline. Initially they are processed from the same raw material, crude oil, but after split-off, they are further processed separately. Additional information is as follows:

	Kerosene	Gasoline	Final Sales
Ultimate sales value................................	$9,000	$6,000	$15,000
Joint costs prior to split-off point............	?	?	6,600
Costs after split-off point	3,600	2,400	6,000

Using the market value method, the assigned joint costs of kerosene and gasoline, respectively, are:
a. $3,300 and $3,300
b. $3,960 and $2,640
c. $4,400 and $2,200
d. $4,560 and $2,040

Part IV

Meridian Manufacturing, Inc. manufactures a single product on a continuous plan in three departments. On June 1, the work in process in the Assembly Department was:

Cost in preceding department	$25,000
Materials—Assembly....................................	–0–
Labor—Assembly	$2,720
Factory overhead—Assembly........................	$1,360
Units in process	5,000

Costs in Assembly during June were:

Materials...	$10,000
Labor..	$25,000
Factory overhead	$12,500

During June, 45,000 units were received from the Machining Department at a cost of $225,000; 40,000 units were completed in Assembly, of which 38,000 were transferred to the Painting Department, and 2,000 were on hand in Assembly at the end of the month. Ten thousand units were still in process, estimated to be one-half complete as to labor and factory overhead. All materials are added at the end of the process in Assembly.

Instructions: Complete the following cost of production report for Assembly, using the average costing method for beginning work-in-process inventories. (Round unit costs to three decimal places.)

Hint: First complete the equivalent production schedule before attempting to compute the unit cost of work added during the period.

Meridian Manufacturing, Inc.
Cost of Production Summary—Assembly
For the Month of June, 2002

Cost of work in process, beginning of month:

   Cost in Machining .... $

   Cost in Assembly:

      Materials...................................... $

      Labor...

      Factory overhead..........................   _____   _____ $

Cost of goods received from Machining during month ..

Cost of production for month:

   Materials .... $

   Labor..

   Factory overhead ....   _____   _____

Total costs to be accounted for .... $

Unit output for month:

Materials ....

    Finished and transferred to Painting during month

    Equivalent units of work in process, end of month

    Finished and on hand ....

        Total equivalent production ....

Labor and factory overhead:

    Finished and transferred to Painting during month

    Equivalent units of work in process, end of month

    Finished and on hand ....

        Total equivalent production ....

Unit cost for month:

Materials .... $

Labor ....

Factory overhead ....

    Total .... $

Inventory costs:

Cost of goods finished and transferred to Painting
during month:

    Cost in Machining .... $

    Cost in Assembly .... $

Cost of work in process, end of month:

Finished and on hand:

    Cost in Machining .... $

    Cost in Assembly ....

Still in process:

    Cost in Machining .... $

    Cost in Assembly:

        Materials.................................... $

        Labor ....

        Factory overhead.......................

Total production cost accounted for .... $

Total cost from preceding dept.:

Work in process—beginning inventory .... $

Transferred in during period......................................

    Total .... $

Total units from preceding dept.:

Work in process—beginning inventory ....

Transferred in during period......................................

    Total ....

Part V

Chavez Chemical Company operates three producing departments—Mixing, Refining, and Finishing. During May, the Refining Department transferred 40,000 units to the Finishing Department and had 7,000 units in process at the end of May. There were 10,000 units in process on May 1 in the Refining Department. The remaining 37,000 units started in the Refining Department during May were received from the Mixing Department. The costs incurred in the Refining Department during May were labor, $50,375, and factory overhead, $40,300. (No materials were added in the Refining Department.) The work-in-process inventory on May 1 was $10,000. The costs transferred to the Refining Department from the Mixing Department amounted to $120,050. The Refining Department work-in-process inventory was one-half complete on May 1 and three-fourths complete on May 31.

Instructions: Complete the following May cost of production report for the Refining Department, using the first-in, first-out method of accounting for beginning inventories. (Carry unit cost computations to three decimal places.)

Chavez Chemical Company
Cost of Production Summary—Refining Department
For the Month of May, 2002

Cost of work in process, beginning of month		$
Cost of goods received from prior department during month		
Cost of production for month:		
Materials	$	
Labor..		
Factory overhead	_____	_____
Total costs to be accounted for		$_____

Unit output for month:

    To complete beginning units in process............................

    Units started and finished during month..........................

    Ending units in process...   _____

       Total equivalent production ....   ========

Unit cost for month:

    Labor... $

    Factory overhead ....   _____

       Total .... $_____

Inventory costs:

    Cost of goods finished and transferred to Finishing
       Department during month:

       Beginning units in process:

          Prior month's cost .... $

          Current cost to complete:

             Labor (_____) ....

             Factory overhead (_____)...   _____ $

       Units started and finished during month:

       Cost in prior department (_____) $

       Cost in Refining Department

          (_____) ....   _____

          Total cost transferred (_____).

    Cost of work in process, end of month:

       Cost in prior department (_____).... $

       Cost in Refining Department:

          Labor (_____)............................

          Factory overhead (_____) ....   _____   _____

Total production costs accounted for................................... $_____

Part VI

Grecian Chemical Company produces two liquid products from one process. The products, Sigma and Chi, are drawn off separately from a huge vat and piped into tank cars for shipment. The joint materials, labor, and overhead costs to produce 15,000 gallons of Sigma and 10,000 gallons of Chi total $100,000. The sales values are $10 per gallon of Sigma and $5 per gallon of Chi.

Instructions:

1. Compute the assignment of joint costs to the individual products using the relative sales value method.

2. Compute the assignment of joint costs to the individual products using the adjusted sales value method, assuming that the costs after split-off are $3 per gallon for Sigma and $1 per gallon for Chi. (Round percentages to two decimal places.)

3. Assume the same facts as in (2) above except that a by-product, Gamma, results from the same process and can be sold for $10,000 without further processing. Compute the assignment of joint costs using the adjusted sales value method and treating the by-product value as a reduction in cost of the main product.

CHAPTER 7 STANDARD COST ACCOUNTING— MATERIALS AND LABOR

Review Summary

1. The purpose of standard cost accounting is to control costs and promote efficiency. Standard costs usually are determined for a period of one year and revised annually. A **standard** is a norm against which performance can be measured. Some companies use **ideal standards** that make no allowance for inefficient conditions such as lost time, waste, or spoilage. Most companies realize that some inefficiencies cannot be completely eliminated, so they use **attainable standards** that include allowances for lost time, spoilage, and waste. The standard should be high enough to provide motivation and promote efficiency, but not so high that it is unattainable and, thus, discourages workers.

2. A **materials cost standard** represents the quantity of material required for a unit of product times the unit cost that should be paid. A **labor cost standard** is based on estimates of the labor hours required to produce a unit of product times the hourly rate that should be paid. Factors to be considered in setting standards for materials and labor might include raw materials price trends, the use of substitute materials, labor negotiations with unions, and the use of labor-saving devices. Once the standard cost of manufacturing a product has been determined, the standard costs, the actual costs, and the variances are recorded in the various journals and in the general ledger.

3. A **variance** represents the difference between the actual and the standard costs of materials, labor, and overhead. The **materials price variance** is computed by comparing the actual unit cost of materials to the standard unit cost, and multiplying the difference by the actual quantity of materials used. The **materials quantity variance** is computed by comparing the actual quantity of materials used to the standard quantity that should have been used, and multiplying the difference by the standard unit price. The **labor rate variance** is computed by comparing the actual hourly rate paid to the standard hourly rate that should have been paid, and multiplying the difference by the actual number of hours worked. The **labor efficiency variance** is computed by comparing the actual number of direct labor hours worked to the standard hours that should have been worked, and multiplying the difference by the standard labor rate. A debit balance (unfavorable) in a variance account indicates that actual costs exceed standard costs, and a credit balance (favorable) means that standard costs exceed actual costs.

4. Sample entries for a standard cost system follow:

   a. To record the entry for direct materials cost, assuming a favorable quantity variance and an unfavorable price variance:

Work in Process (at standard cost).............................	XX	
Materials Price Variance	XX	
Materials Quantity Variance..................................		XX
Materials (at actual cost)		XX

    b. To record the entry for direct labor cost, assuming a favorable rate variance and an unfavorable efficiency variance:

Work in Process (at standard cost)............................	XX	
Labor Efficiency Variance	XX	
Labor Rate Variance		XX
Payroll (at actual cost)...		XX

    c. To record the entry applying factory overhead to work in process, assuming no variances:

Work in Process..	XX	
Applied Factory Overhead		XX

    d. To record the transfer, at standard cost, of work in process to finished goods:

Finished Goods...	XX	
Work in Process		XX

At the end of the accounting period, the difference between actual costs and standard costs must be reflected in the financial statements. Some companies prorate the variances to cost of goods sold, work in process, and finished goods. A more common approach is to show the unfavorable or favorable variances as an addition to or reduction from the cost of goods sold for the period, respectively.

5. In analyzing materials and labor variances, both **price** and **usage** have to be considered. In analyzing materials price variances, inefficient purchasing methods, the substitution of different materials, and increases in market price are all possible explanations. In analyzing materials quantity variances, possible explanations include spoiled or wasted materials and the decision to use higher quality materials subsequent to the budget preparation. In analyzing labor rate variances, changes in labor wage rates subsequent to standard-setting and the use of employees with wage rates different from those called for in the standards are possible reasons. In analyzing labor efficiency variances, the skill level of workers, the frequency of machine breakdowns, and improper scheduling should all be considered.

6. Things to remember about standard cost systems are that:

    a. the actual unit cost of manufacturing a product is not determined—only the total actual and total standard costs.

    b. the fact that standards are based on estimates does not make them unreliable.

    c. standards will change as conditions change.

    d. a standard cost system provides continual incentive to keep costs and performance in line with predetermined objectives.

    e. a standard cost system helps focus management's attention on prices paid for materials and labor and on materials and labor quantity usage.

    f. to allow for more timely action in correcting inefficiencies, most manufacturers calculate variances on a weekly or even daily basis.

Part I

Instructions: Indicate your answer in the Answers column by writing a "T" for True or an "F" for False.

Answers

1. Standard costs are usually determined for a period of one year............. _____

2. "Ideal standards" include allowances for lost time, spoilage, and waste. _____

3. In establishing standard costs, the standard should be high enough to provide motivation and promote efficiency, but not so high that it is unattainable. .... _____

4. The materials price variance is computed by comparing the actual unit cost of materials to the standard unit cost, and multiplying the difference by the standard quantity of materials used....................... _____

5. A variance is favorable if the actual cost incurred is greater than the standard cost allowed...................... _____

6. A debit balance in a variance account indicates that standard costs exceed actual costs....................... _____

7. A method of disposing of the difference between actual costs and standard costs prior to financial statement preparation is to close the variance accounts to Cost of Goods Sold. .... _____

8. Inefficient purchasing methods, the substitution of different materials, and increases in market price are all possible explanations for materials price variances....................... _____

9. The skill level of workers, the frequency of machine breakdowns, and improper scheduling are all possible reasons for labor rate variances. .... _____

10. The actual unit cost of manufacturing a product is not determined using a standard cost system....................... _____

11. The standards used in a standard cost system will change as conditions change....................... _____

12. The fact that standards are based on estimates tends to make a standard cost system unreliable. .... _____

13. A standard cost system can be used in conjunction with process costing or job order costing. .... _____

14. In a standard cost system, the entry to record the issuance of materials into production would include a debit to Work in Process for the actual cost of the materials. .... _____

15. Some companies reflect the difference between actual and standard costs in the financial statements by prorating the variances to Cost of Goods Sold, Work in Process, and Finished Goods. .... _____

Part II

Instructions: In the Answers column, place the letter from the list below that identifies the term that best matches the statement. No letter should be used more than once.

a. Attainable standard
b. Favorable variance
c. Materials price variance
d. Materials usage variance
e. Ideal standard
f. Standard

g. Labor rate variance
h. Labor cost standard
i. Materials cost standard
j. Unfavorable variance
k. Labor efficiency variance
l. Learning effect
m. Management by exception

Answers

_____ 1. This is the explanation as to why employees become more proficient at a task the more often that they perform it.

_____ 2. This is represented by a debit balance in a variance account.

_____ 3. A norm against which performance can be measured.

_____ 4. It can be achieved only under the most efficient operating conditions, and for all practical purposes it is unattainable.

_____ 5. Some inefficiencies were built into this so that it can be met or bettered in efficient production situations.

_____ 6. This represents the quantity of material required for a unit of product times the cost per unit of material.

_____ 7. In determining this, the services of work-study engineers may be used to establish the time necessary to perform each operation.

_____ 8. This is represented by a credit balance in a variance account.

_____ 9. This indicates the number of actual direct labor hours worked above or below the standard times the standard labor rate.

_____ 10. This indicates the actual unit cost of materials above or below the standard unit cost, multiplied by the actual quantity of materials used.

_____ 11. This represents the average of the actual hourly direct labor rates paid above or below the standard hourly rate, multiplied by the actual number of hours worked.

_____ 12. This represents the actual quantity of direct materials used above or below the standard quantity allowed for the actual level of production times the standard price.

_____ 13. This is the practice of examining those occurrences which vary greatly from the norm.

Part III

Instructions: In the Answers column, place the letter of the choice that most correctly completes each item.

Answers

_____ 1. The best basis upon which cost standards should be set to measure controllable production efficiencies is:
   a. Theoretical standards
   b. Expected actual standards
   c. Attainable standards
   d. Practical capacity

_____ 2. If a company follows a practice of isolating variances at the earliest time, the appropriate time to isolate and recognize a direct material price variance would be:
   a. When material is issued
   b. When material is purchased
   c. When material is used in production
   d. When the purchase order is originated

_____ 3. Practical Company manufactures tables with vinyl tops. The standard material cost for the vinyl used for one type of table is $7.80, based on six square feet of vinyl at a cost of $1.30 per square foot. A production run of 1,000 tables in January resulted in usage of 6,400 square feet of vinyl at a cost of $1.20 per square foot, for a total cost of $7,680. The materials quantity variance resulting from this production run was:
   a. $120 favorable
   b. $520 unfavorable
   c. $480 unfavorable
   d. $640 favorable

_____ 4. Actual units of direct materials used were 20,000, at an actual cost of $40,000. Standard unit cost is $2.10. The materials price variance is:
   a. $1,000 favorable
   b. $1,000 unfavorable
   c. $2,000 favorable
   d. $2,000 unfavorable

_____ 5. Information on Gerhardt Company's direct labor costs for the month of January follows:

Actual direct labor hours	34,500
Standard direct labor hours...................	35,000
Total direct labor payroll	$241,500
Standard direct labor rate......................	$6.40

Gerhardt's direct labor rate variance is:
   a. $17,250 unfavorable
   b. $20,700 unfavorable
   c. $21,000 unfavorable
   d. $21,000 favorable

_____ 6. The direct labor standards for producing a unit of a product are two hours at $10 per hour. Budgeted production was 1,000 units. Actual production was 900 units, and direct labor cost was $19,000 for 2,000 direct labor hours. The direct labor efficiency variance was:
   a. $1,000 favorable
   b. $1,000 unfavorable
   c. $2,000 favorable
   d. $2,000 unfavorable

_____ **7.** Of the following, the most probable reason a company would experience an unfavorable labor rate variance and a favorable labor efficiency variance is that:

    a. The mix of workers assigned to the particular job was weighted heavily towards the use of higher paid, experienced individuals

    b. The mix of workers assigned to the particular job was weighted heavily towards the use of new, relatively low paid, unskilled workers

    c. Because of the production schedule, workers from other production areas were assigned to assist this particular process

    d. Defective materials caused more labor to be used in order to produce a standard unit

_____ **8.** A debit balance in the labor-efficiency variance account indicates that:

    a. Standard hours exceed actual hours

    b. Actual hours exceed standard hours

    c. Standard rate and standard hours exceed actual rate and actual hours

    d. Actual rate and actual hours exceed standard rate and standard hours

_____ **9.** How should a usage variance that is significant in amount be treated at the end of an accounting period?

    a. Reported as a deferred charge or credit

    b. Allocated among work-in-process inventory, finished goods inventory, and cost of goods sold

    c. Charged or credited to cost of goods manufactured

    d. Allocated among cost of goods manufactured, finished goods inventory, and cost of goods sold

_____ **10.** The following journal entry has been recorded:

Work in Process	10,000	
Labor Rate Variance	2,000	
Labor Efficiency Variance		1,000
Payroll		11,000

This entry indicates that:

a. Actual labor cost is less than standard labor cost

b. The labor rate variance is favorable

c. The labor efficiency variance is unfavorable

d. Actual labor cost is more than standard labor cost

Part IV

Merkle Company has a budgeted normal monthly capacity of 20,000 labor hours with a standard production of 10,000 units at this capacity. Standard costs are as follows:

Materials .... 3 lbs. @ $1
Labor .... $15 per hour

During March, 19,500 actual labor hours cost $282,750, and 9,500 units were produced using 29,200 pounds of materials at a cost of $1.10 per pound.

Instructions:

1. Compute the materials cost variances and label each as favorable or unfavorable.

	Pounds	Unit Cost		Amount
Actual quantity used...............		$	Actual	$
Actual quantity used...............		_____	Standard	_____
Materials price variance..........		$_____		$_____
Actual quantity used...............		$	Standard	$
Standard quantity allowed.......	_____		Standard	_____
Materials quantity variance.....	_____			$_____

2. Compute the labor cost variances and label each as favorable or unfavorable.

	Time	Rate		Amount
Actual hours worked...............		$	Actual	$
Actual hours worked...............		_____	Standard	_____
Labor rate variance.................		$_____		$_____
Actual hours worked...............		$	Standard	$
Standard hours allowed...........	_____		Standard	_____
Labor efficiency variance........	_____			$_____

3. Prepare the same variance analysis as above, using the diagram format as illustrated in Figure 7-1 of the text.

Name _____

Part V

Alfred Corp., which uses a standard cost accounting system, determines that the following variances arose in production during June:

Variance	Amount
Materials purchase price	$ 900 favorable
Materials quantity...........................	750 unfavorable
Labor efficiency..............................	1,000 unfavorable
Labor rate.......................................	600 unfavorable

Direct materials purchases totaled $90,000 at standard cost, while $75,000 in materials were taken from inventory for use in production. Actual direct labor totaled $80,000, while actual overhead incurred was $60,000. (Assume no variance for factory overhead.) Ten thousand units were transferred to Finished Goods at a standard cost of $15 per unit.

Instructions: Prepare the journal entries to record:

1. The purchase of materials (The materials price variance is recorded at the time of purchase.)
2. The use of materials in production
3. The use of labor in production
4. The charging of overhead to production
5. The transfer of finished goods to the storeroom

Account	Debit	Credit
(1)		
(2)		
(3)		
(4)		
(5)		

Part VI

From the following list of account titles and balances, prepare an income statement through gross margin for the Verdin Co. for the year ended December 31, 2002.

Account	Balance (dr. or cr.)
Materials Price Variance	$ 820 dr.
Sales	80,000 cr.
Labor Efficiency Variance	200 cr.
Materials Quantity Variance	1,600 cr.
Cost of Goods Sold at Standard	50,000 dr.
Labor Rate Variance	210 dr.

CHAPTER 8 BUDGETING AND STANDARD COST ACCOUNTING FOR FACTORY OVERHEAD

Review Summary

1. A **budget** is a planning device that enables companies to set goals and to measure results against those goals. It is a chart of the course of operations that forecasts costs and profits and that aids managers in controlling costs and analyzing company strengths and weaknesses. The general principles of budgeting include clearly defined objectives; realistic goals; consideration of economic developments, the general business climate, industry conditions, and changes and trends; comparison of actual results to budget; flexibility to modify in light of changing conditions; and the affixing of responsibility for forecasting costs and accountability for results.

2. The **sales budget** projects the volume of sales for the coming period in both units and dollars, and is used as the basis for the preparation of all other budgets. The **production budget** determines the units to be produced by adding the desired ending inventory to the units estimated to be sold, and then subtracting the beginning inventory. The **budgets for direct materials, direct labor, and factory overhead** for the coming period are based on the required production from the production schedule. The **cost of goods sold budget** may be prepared upon completion of the above budgets. Once the level of activity has been determined for sales and production, the **selling and administrative expenses budget** can be prepared. Completion of these individual budgets permits the preparation of the **budgeted income statement**. The **cash budget** shows the estimated flow of cash and the timing of receipts and disbursements based on projected revenues, the production schedule, and the estimated expenses. The **capital expenditures budget** is a plan for the timing of acquisitions of buildings, equipment, and other significant assets.

3. A **flexible budget** shows the planned expenses at various levels of production. Using flexible budgeting, management quickly can determine variances by comparing actual costs with what the costs of production should have been at the actual level of production. In preparing a flexible budget for factory overhead, a company must first determine the **standard production** on which the initial calculation of costs is based. In making this determination one may use **theoretical capacity**, which represents the maximum number of units that can be produced under ideal circumstances; **practical capacity**, which assumes complete utilization of all facilities and personnel, but allows for some idle capacity due to operating interruptions; or **normal capacity**, the most often used production level, which allows for both unavoidable idle capacity due to lack of demand and some inefficiencies in operations.

4. In examining a flexible budget you will notice that the factory overhead per unit decreases as volume increases because the fixed factory overhead is being spread over more production. If actual production is the same as normal production for a period, any variance will be a budget or controllable variance rather than a volume variance. **Semifixed** or **step costs**, such as supervisory salaries, tend to remain fixed in dollar amount through a certain range of activity but increase when production exceeds

certain limits. **Semivariable** factory overhead costs, such as electricity expense or training costs, tend to vary with production but not in direct proportion.

5. The **two-variance method, three-variance method**, and **four-variance method** commonly are used for analyzing overhead variances. The two variances in the two-variance method are the controllable or budget variance and the volume variance. The **controllable variance** is the difference between the actual overhead for a given period and the standard amount of overhead allowed by the budget for that level of production. If the actual overhead exceeds the standard overhead allowed, the difference is called an **unfavorable variance**, and if the actual overhead is less than the standard allowed, the difference is called a **favorable variance**.

6. The **volume variance** is a result of operating at a level of production different from the standard, or normal, level. Because fixed costs will remain about the same, in total, whether production is above or below standard, the volume variance will be favorable if actual production exceeds standard and unfavorable if actual production is less than standard. If the factory is producing below its normal capacity, it has idle capacity that nevertheless requires expenditures for depreciation, insurance, property taxes, etc.

7. The **net variance** is the difference between the actual factory overhead for the period and the standard overhead costs applied to work in process. Using the two-variance method, the net variance may be subdivided into its two components as follows:

> Volume variance = (production for period × standard factory overhead unit cost) – standard factory overhead budgeted for period's production
>
> Controllable variance = standard factory overhead budgeted for the period's production – actual factory overhead.

The reasons for the individual variances should be investigated. For example, an unfavorable volume variance may be the result of either production inefficiencies, such as machine breakdowns and unskilled laborers, or it may be due to a lack of product demand, which would be the responsibility of marketing and sales. An unfavorable controllable variance may be the result of unanticipated price increases, inefficient supervision, weak control of expenditures, or increased maintenance and repair costs caused by utilization of production facilities beyond normal capacity.

8. The four-variance method recognizes two variable cost variances and two fixed cost variances. The variable cost variances are identified as a spending variance and an efficiency variance. For fixed cost, a budget variance and a volume variance is determined. The controllable variance under the two-variance method encompasses the spending, efficiency, and budget variance of the four-variance method. The volume variance is a separate item under both methods.

9. The three-variance method of factory overhead cost analysis breaks down the difference between actual and applied overhead into the following variances: the **efficiency variance** measures the difference between the overhead applied (standard hours × standard rate) and the actual hours worked, multiplied by the standard rate; the **capacity variance** reflects the under- or over-absorption of fixed costs and is measured by the difference between the actual hours worked, multiplied by the standard overhead rate and the budget allowance based on actual hours worked; and the **budget (spending) variance**, which reflects the difference between the amount allowed by the budget for the actual hours worked and the actual costs incurred. Whether the two-, three-, or four-variance method of overhead analysis is used, the overhead applied to production, the actual overhead, and the net variance would be the same.

Part I

Instructions: Indicate your answer in the Answers column by writing a "T" for True or an "F" for False.

Answers

1. Budgeting encompasses the coordination and control of every item on the balance sheet and income statement.. _____

2. Once the direct materials budget has been prepared, the production budget can be prepared.. .... _____

3. The sales budget is especially important because management must use its information to prepare all other budgets.. _____

4. The cost of goods sold budget may be prepared upon completion of the direct materials, direct labor and factory overhead budgets .... _____

5. A flexible budget is useful because it shows the planned expenses at various levels of production.. _____

6. Most manufacturing firms use normal capacity for budget development because it represents a logical balance between maximum capacity and the capacity demanded by actual sales volume...................................... _____

7. Theoretical capacity represents a production level that is almost impossible to attain. .... _____

8. Step costs are those that tend to remain the same in dollar amount through a certain range of activity, but increase when production exceeds certain limits.. _____

9. The preparation of a budget for a service department follows the same procedure as that for a production department.. _____

10. The primary difference between the two-variance and three-variance methods of variance analysis is that the three-variance method determines the budget allowance based on actual hours worked rather than on standard hours. .... _____

11. The two-variance method of analyzing overhead variances is the most commonly used approach. .... _____

12. A debit balance in the factory overhead account indicates that the factory did not incur as much overhead as was allowed by the standard at that level of production. .... _____

13. An unfavorable volume variance may be the result of inefficiencies in labor and supervision, machine breakdowns due to faulty maintenance, and even lack of sales demand.. _____

14. When factory overhead is applied to production, Factory Overhead is debited and Work in Process is credited. .... _____

15. On the financial statements, overhead variances usually are treated as additions to or subtractions from cost of goods sold............................... _____

Part II

Instructions: In the Answers column, place the letter from the list below that identifies the term that best matches the statement. No letter should be used more than once.

a. Capital expenditures budget
b. Controllable variance
c. Cash budget
d. Variable costs

e. Fixed costs
f. Sales budget
g. Budgeted income statement

h. Theoretical capacity
i. Step costs
j. Capacity variance
k. Efficiency variance
l. Flexible budget

m. Two-variance method
n. Normal capacity

o. Practical capacity
p. Four-variance method
q. Volume variance
r. Semivariable costs
s. Cost of goods sold budget manufacturing costs
t. Budget variance

Answers

_____ 1. This is the most commonly used approach to variance analysis.

_____ 2. To compute this, a comparison must be made between the actual factory overhead for a given period and the standard amount of overhead allowed by the budget at a given level of production.

_____ 3. It results from operating at a level of production different from the standard, or normal, level.

_____ 4. These tend to remain the same in dollar amount through a certain range of activity but increase when production exceeds certain limits.

_____ 5. This summarizes the data from all other budgets and enables management to determine the impact of all budget estimates on profit.

_____ 6. Management must use this budget as a basis for planning all other budgets.

_____ 7. This includes the estimated costs of materials, labor, and factory overhead as well as estimates of beginning and ending inventories of work in process and finished goods.

_____ 8. This shows the anticipated flow of cash and the timing of receipts and disbursements based upon projected revenues, the production schedule, and expenses.

_____ 9. These may change with the level of production, but not necessarily in direct proportion.

_____ 10. This is a plan for the timing of acquisition of buildings, equipment, or other significant assets.

_____ 11. By using this, management can quickly determine variances by comparing actual costs with what the costs of production should have been for the level achieved.

_____ 12. Costs that do not change as production changes over a given range.

_____ 13. These are a function of activity and include direct labor and direct materials.

_____ 14. This method of variance analysis identifies a spending variance and an efficiency variance for variable costs.

_____ **15.** This represents the maximum number of units that can be produced with the completely efficient use of all available facilities and personnel.

_____ **16.** This is the level of production that provides complete utilization of facilities and personnel, but allows for some idle capacity due to operating interruptions.

_____ **17.** This level of capacity does not involve a plan for maximum usage of operating facilities, but allows for some unavoidable idle capacity and inefficiencies in operations.

_____ **18.** In the three-variance method, this measures the difference between the overhead applied (standard hours at the standard rate) and the actual hours worked, multiplied by the standard rate.

_____ **19.** In the three-variance method, this is measured by the difference between the actual hours worked, multiplied by the standard overhead rate and the budget allowance based on actual hours worked.

_____ **20.** In the four-variance method, this measures the difference between actual fixed cost expenditures and the amount of fixed cost budgeted.

Part III

Instructions: In the Answers column, place the letter of the choice that most correctly completes each item.

Answers

_____ **1.** Overapplied factory overhead would result if:
   a. The plant was operated at less than normal capacity
   b. Factory overhead costs incurred were less than costs charged to production
   c. Factory overhead costs incurred were unreasonably large in relation to units produced
   d. Factory overhead costs incurred were greater than costs charged to production

_____ **2.** Under the two-variance method for analyzing factory overhead, the factory overhead applied to production is used in the computation of:

	Controllable (Budget) Variance	**Volume Variance**
a.	Yes	No
b.	Yes	Yes
c.	No	Yes
d.	No	No

_____ **3.** A spending variance for factory overhead is the difference between actual factory overhead cost and factory overhead cost that should have been incurred for the actual hours worked. It results from:
   a. Price differences for factory overhead costs
   b. Quantity differences for factory overhead costs
   c. Price and quantity differences for factory overhead costs
   d. Differences caused by production volume variation

4. A company found that the difference in product costs that resulted from the application of predetermined factory overhead rates, rather than actual factory overhead rates, were immaterial, even though actual production was substantially less than planned production. The most likely explanation is that:
a. Factory overhead was composed chiefly of variable costs
b. Several products were produced simultaneously
c. Fixed factory overhead was a significant cost
d. Costs of factory overhead items were substantially larger than anticipated

5. Under the two-variance method for analyzing factory overhead, the difference between the actual factory overhead and the factory overhead applied to production is the:
a. Controllable variance
b. Net overhead variance
c. Efficiency variance
d. Volume variance

6. Which of the following budgets is influenced more directly by the sales budget than by the production budget?
a. Direct materials budget
b. Selling and administrative expenses budget
c Direct labor budget
d. Factory overhead budget

7. When using a flexible budget, as production decreases within the relevant range, fixed costs:
a. Will decrease per unit
b. Will remain unchanged per unit
c. Will increase per unit
d. Are not considered in flexible budgeting

Items 8 and 9 are based on the following information:

The data below relate to the month of May for Moreno Inc., which uses a standard cost system and two-variance analysis of overhead:

Actual total direct labor	$43,400
Actual hours used	14,000
Standard hours allowed for good output	15,000
Direct labor rate variance—debit	$1,400
Actual total overhead	$40,250
Budgeted fixed costs	$9,000
"Normal" activity in hours	18,000
Total overhead application rate per standard direct labor hour	$3.00

8. What was Moreno's volume variance for May?
a. $1,250 favorable
b. $1,250 unfavorable
c. $1,500 favorable
d. $1,500 unfavorable

9. What was Moreno's controllable variance for May?
a. $1,250 favorable
b. $6,250 favorable
c. $1,500 favorable
d. $1,500 unfavorable

_____ **10.** The following information is available from the Maris Company:

Actual factory overhead	$7,500
Fixed overhead expenses, actual.....................................	$3,600
Fixed overhead expenses, budgeted..............................	$3,500
Actual hours...	1,750
Standard hours..	300
Variable overhead rate per direct labor hour	$1.25

Assuming that Maris uses a three-variance analysis of overhead, what is the spending variance?

a. $1,812.50 favorable   c. $3,625 unfavorable

b. $1,812.50 unfavorable   d. $100 unfavorable

Part IV

Instructions: The format for a flexible overhead budget follows. Compute the amount that should be budgeted for each indicated level of activity by completing the schedule, then compute the overall factory overhead rate and the fixed factory overhead rate per direct labor hour carried to three decimal places.

Factory Expense Category	Budget Rate	Level of Activity (Direct Labor Hours)			
		45,000	50,000	55,000	60,000
Variable costs (per direct labor hour):					
Indirect labor.....................	$2.00	$	$	$	$
Indirect materials..............	.80				
Repairs	.60	_____	_____	_____	_____
Total variable cost	$3.40	$_____	$_____	$_____	$_____
Fixed costs (total):					
Depreciation—machinery	$50,000	$	$	$	$
Insurance—factory	25,000	_____	_____	_____	_____
Total fixed cost.............	$75,000	$_____	$_____	$_____	$_____
Total overhead budget...........		$_____	$_____	$_____	$_____
Factory overhead rate per direct labor hour		$_____	$_____	$_____	$_____
Fixed overhead rate per direct labor hour		$_____	$_____	$_____	$_____

Part V

Factory overhead for Wellington Company has been estimated as follows:

Fixed factory overhead	$50,000
Variable factory overhead	$100,000
Estimated direct labor hours	20,000

Production for the month reached 110% of the budget, and actual factory overhead totaled $163,000.

Instructions:

1. Determine the over- or underapplied factory overhead.

Actual factory overhead	$
Applied factory overhead	
Over- or underapplied factory overhead	$

2. Determine the controllable and volume variances.

Actual factory overhead		$
Overhead for capacity attained:		
Fixed factory overhead	$	
Variable factory overhead		
Controllable variance		$
Factory overhead for capacity attained		$
Factory overhead applied		
Volume variance		$

Part VI

Bass Company has a budgeted normal monthly capacity of 20,000 labor hours, with a standard production of 10,000 units at this capacity. Standard costs for factory overhead are as follows:

Factory overhead at normal capacity:
Fixed... $20,000
Variable... $5 per labor hour

During March, actual factory overhead totaled $117,000, of which $97,000 was for variable overhead; and 19,500 labor hours were required to produce 9,500 units.

Instructions:

1. Compute the factory overhead variances using the two-variance method.

Actual factory overhead...		$
Budget allowance based on standard hours allowed:		
Fixed overhead budgeted...	$	
Variable overhead	_____	_____
Controllable variance		$_____
Budget allowance based on standard hours allowed...		$
Overhead charged to production.................................		_____
Volume variance		$_____

2. Compute the factory overhead variances using the four-variance method (appendix).

Actual variable factory overhead..	$
Budget allowance based on actual hours worked:	
Variable overhead	_____
Spending variance	$_____
Actual hours × standard variable overhead rate	$
Variable overhead charged to production	_____
Efficiency variance	$_____
Actual fixed cost	$
Budgeted fixed cost..	_____
Budget variance	$_____
Budgeted fixed cost..	$
Standard hours × fixed rate...	_____
Volume variance	$_____

Part VII

Fashion Outlet Inc. prepared the following figures as a basis for its 2002 budget:

Product	Expected Sales	Estimated Sales Price per Unit	Required Materials per Unit Rayon	Cotton
Socks	50,000 units	$5	4 lbs.	2 lbs.
Shorts	25,000	8	5 lbs.	–
Handkerchiefs	75,000	3	–	3 lbs.

Estimated inventories at the beginning and desired quantities at the end of 2002 are:

Material	Beginning	Ending	Purchase Price per Pound
Rayon	6,000 lbs.	7,500 lbs.	$.75
Cotton	5,000	6,000	.50

Product	Beginning	Ending
Socks	3,000 units	2,500 units
Shorts	1,000	2,000
Handkerchiefs	4,000	5,000

Instructions:

1. Prepare the production budget.

	Socks	Shorts	Handkerchiefs
Units required to meet sales budget	_____	_____	_____
Add desired ending inventories	_____	_____	_____
Total units required	_____	_____	_____
Less estimated beginning inventories	_____	_____	_____
Planned production	_____	_____	_____

2. Prepare the direct materials budget.

	Rayon	Cotton
Socks	_____	_____
Shorts	_____	_____
Handkerchiefs	_____	_____
Total	_____	_____
Add desired ending inventories	_____	_____
Total	_____	_____
Less estimated beginning inventories	_____	_____
Budgeted quantities of materials purchases	_____	_____
Budgeted purchase price per pound	× _____	× _____
Budgeted dollar amounts of materials purchases	$ _____	$ _____

CHAPTER 9 COST ACCOUNTING FOR SERVICE BUSINESSES

Review Summary

1. A **service** is an intangible benefit, such as consulting, designing, grooming, transporting, and entertaining. It does not have physical properties, and it is consumed at the time that it is provided. It cannot be saved or stored and therefore is not inventoried. Service businesses are important because roughly 70% of U.S. workers are employed by service businesses, which account for more than 60% of the value of the total production of goods and services in this country. Approximately 90% of the jobs created in the U.S. in the last 20 years have been in service industries. Knowing the cost of providing services is important to managers for such purposes as contract bidding and deciding what services to emphasize or de-emphasize in their line of offerings.

2. The amount and complexity of services provided can vary substantially from customer to customer. When this is the case, a service firm should use **job order costing**, just as the manufacturer of differentiated products uses such a system. The basic document used to accumulate costs for a service business using job order costing is the **job order cost sheet**, which also is used in our manufacturing examples. Because direct labor cost usually is the single largest cost to a service firm and the need for these direct laborers results in all the other costs the firm incurs, the amount of direct labor cost incurred on a job determines how much overhead will be charged to it. There are costs other than direct labor, such as travel and meal charges, that can be traced to a job. These expenses, specifically identified with the job, do not have to be allocated to the job using an overhead rate. Once a job is completed and all of the costs have been charged to it, management can use the information in a number of ways. It can compare the costs charged to a job with the bid price accepted by the client to determine the profitability of the job. It can use the information for bidding on the same or similar jobs in the future and for comparing budgeted to actual costs for the purpose of controlling future costs.

3. The **revenue budget** is the starting point for the annual budget because the amount of client business must be projected before the amount of labor hours needed and overhead incurred can be estimated. The billing rates reflect the firm's best estimate of what it will charge clients for the various categories of professional labor in the coming year. Once the amount of professional labor hours required to meet client services is budgeted, a **professional labor budget** may be prepared. The budgeted hours required in each client service area are multiplied by the budgeted rate to obtain the wages expense for each category of professional labor. The firm must next prepare an **overhead budget** that includes all of the expense items that cannot be traced directly to jobs, but must be allocated to them by using an overhead rate. The last of the individual budgets for a firm would be the **other expenses budget**, which consists of the direct expenses other than professional labor, such as meals and travel, that can be traced to specific jobs. Once all of the individual budgets have been prepared, the information they contain can be used to prepare the budgeted income statement.

4. Firms that use **activity-based costing** (ABC) attempt to shift as many costs as possible out of the indirect cost pool, which has to be allocated to jobs, and into direct cost pools, which can be specifically traced to the individual jobs that caused the costs to occur. The remaining costs that cannot be traced to individual jobs are separated into homogeneous cost pools and then allocated to individual jobs by using separate allocation bases for each cost pool. The increased sophistication and affordability of information processing technology enables costs such as telephone, fax, and photocopying, which previously were classified as indirect and included in the overhead rate, to be traced directly to specific jobs at minimal cost. These items, which had previously been "spread like peanut butter" over all the jobs, can now be specifically identified with the jobs that caused these costs to occur. **Peanut-butter costing** refers to the practice of assigning costs evenly to jobs using an overhead rate, when different jobs consume resources in different proportions. The other main ingredient of activity-based costing is to take overhead costs that were previously in a single indirect cost pool and to separate them into a number of homogeneous cost pools with a separate cost driver, or cost allocation base, for each pool.

Part I

Instructions: Indicate your answer in the Answers column by writing a "T" for True or an "F" for False.

Answers

1. A main feature of service businesses is that they have large amounts of inventory. .... _____

2. Approximately 90% of the jobs created in the U.S. in the last twenty years have been in service industries. .... _____

3. Historically, cost accountants have spent most of their time developing costs for service businesses. .... _____

4. The basic document used to accumulate costs for a service business is the job order cost sheet. .... _____

5. Direct labor cost is usually the single largest cost to a service firm. .... _____

6. If all categories of direct labor worked on a job consume the same amount of overhead per hour worked, direct labor hours would be a more appropriate basis to use for charging overhead than direct labor dollars. .... _____

7. A cost performance report compares the actual costs incurred on a job to the budgeted costs and indicates the variance, or difference, for each item. .... _____

8. The professional labor budget is the starting point for the annual budget because labor costs must be known before any other budget items can be projected. .... _____

9. The term "overhead" for a professional services firm has the same meaning as "overhead" for a manufacturer. .... _____

10. Once all of the individual budgets for a service firm have been prepared, the information they contain can be used to prepare a budgeted income statement. .... _____

11. Firms that use ABC attempt to shift as many costs as possible out of the direct cost pool, which has to be allocated to jobs, and into indirect cost pools, which can be traced to individual jobs. .... _____

12. The increased sophistication and affordability of information processing technology enables more costs to be classified as direct and traced to individual jobs. .... _____

13. "Peanut-butter costing" refers to the practice of assigning costs evenly to jobs using an overhead rate, even when different jobs consume resources in different proportions. .... _____

14. It should be a cost/benefit decision for a business in deciding whether to implement a more sophisticated costing system. .... _____

15. An example of a cost driver for the secretarial support cost pool in a law firm would be partner labor hours. .... _____

Part II

Instructions: In the Answers column, place the letter from the list below that identifies the term that best matches the statement. No letter should be used more than once.

a. Job cost sheet
b. Billing rates
c. Activity-based costing
d. Cost performance report
e. Indirect costs

f. Peanut-butter costing
g. Service
h. Budgeted income statement
i. Revenue budget
j. Direct costs

Answers

_____ 1. It does not have physical properties, and it is consumed at the time that it is provided.

_____ 2. It is the basic document used to accumulate costs for a service business.

_____ 3. These represent costs that can be specifically traced to an individual job.

_____ 4. It compares the budgeted costs for a job to the actual costs and indicates a variance for each line item.

_____ 5. It is the starting point for the annual budget.

_____ 6. These represent a firm's best estimate of what it will charge clients for the various categories of professional labor in the coming year.

_____ 7. It can be prepared once all of the individual budgets have been prepared.

_____ 8. It attempts to shift as many costs as possible out of indirect cost pools, which have to be allocated to jobs, and into direct costs pools, which can be specifically traced to individual jobs.

_____ 9. It refers to the practice of assigning costs to jobs evenly using an overhead rate, even though different jobs consume resources in different proportions.

_____ 10. These represent costs that must be allocated to individual jobs via an overhead rate.

Part III

Instructions: In the Answers column, place the letter of the choice that most correctly completes each item.

Answers

_____ 1. The approximate percentage of U.S. workers who are employed in service businesses is:

a. 60%   c. 80%
b. 70%   d. 40%

_____ 2. All of the following are examples of service businesses except:

a. Bottlers
b. Plumbers
c. Consultants
d. Professional sports franchises

_____ 3. What percentage of jobs created in the U.S. in the last 20 years have been in service industries?

a. 60%   c. 80%
b. 70%   d. 90%

_____ 4. The basic document used to accumulate costs for a service business using job order costing is the:

a. Cost performance report
b. Activity-based costing sheet
c. Job order cost sheet
d. Cost/benefit report sheet

_____ 5. In a professional services firm where partners have preferential access to the secretarial support staff, the costs in the secretarial support pool would best be allocated to jobs using:

a. Professional labor dollars
b. Professional labor hours
c. Copy machine hours
d. Professional and nonprofessional labor hours

_____ 6. The individual budget in a professional services firm that is the ending point in the preparation of the annual budget is the:

a. Budgeted income statement
b. Revenue budget
c. Professional labor budget
d. Overhead budget

_____ 7. Examples of direct expenses in a professional services firm that could readily be traced to individual jobs include:

a. Secretarial support
b. Lease expense
c. Utilities
d. Meals and travel

_____ **8.** A report that compares the budgeted costs for a job to the actual costs incurred and indicates the variance for each line item is known as a:
a. Cost/benefit report
b. Variance analysis report
c. Cost performance report
d. Budget

_____ **9.** Firms that use activity-based costing attempt to:
a. Shift as many costs as possible out of indirect cost pools and treat them as direct costs
b. Practice a peanut-butter costing approach to jobs
c. Use a single overhead cost pool whenever possible
d. Shift as many costs as possible from direct cost pools into indirect cost pools

_____ **10.** Peanut-butter costing refers to the practice of:
a. Applying activity-based costing principles to job cost allocations
b. Assigning indirect costs evenly to jobs even when different jobs consume resources in different proportions
c. Having numerous indirect cost pools rather than a single pool
d. Adhering to a cost/benefit approach in determining the number of indirect cost pools

Name _____

Part IV

Billick and Fischer, partners in a management consulting firm, budgeted the following professional labor hours for the year ended December 31, 2002:

Partners	2,000
Associates	7,000
Staff..	11,000

Partners have a billing rate of $200 per hour and actually earn $100 per hour. Associates bill out at $120 per hour and earn $60 per hour. Staff have a billing rate of $80 an hour and earn $40 per hour.

Budgeted overhead and other expenses are as follows:

Overhead:

Depreciation—Equipment...................	$ 40,000
Depreciation—Building.......................	90,000
Fringe Benefits	190,000
Photocopying	22,000
Secretarial Support.............................	230,000
Telephone/Fax....................................	31,000
Utilities..	43,000

Other Expenses:

Travel...	$ 54,000
Meals	18,000

Instructions:

1. Using the schedule below, prepare a revenue budget for the year ended December 31, 2002.

Billick and Fischer
Revenue Budget
For the Year Ended December 31, 2002

Item	Professional Hours	Billing Rate	Total Revenues
Partners.........................		$	$
Associates.....................			
Staff..............................	_____		_____
Total.........................	_____		$_____

2. Using the schedule below, prepare a professional labor budget for the year ended December 31, 2002.

Billick and Fischer
Professional Labor Budget
For the Year Ended December 31, 2002

Item	Professional Hours	Wage Rate	Total Labor Dollars
Partners.........................		$	$
Associates.....................			
Staff..............................	_____		_____
Total.........................	_____		$_____

3. Using the schedule below, prepare an overhead budget for the year ended December 31, 2002.

Billick and Fischer
Overhead Budget
For the Year Ended December 31, 2002

Item	Amount
Secretarial Support	$
Fringe Benefits	
Depreciation—Building	
Utilities	
Depreciation—Equipment	
Telephone/Fax	
Photocopying	
Total	$

4. Using the schedule below, prepare another expenses budget for the year ended December 31, 2002.

Billick and Fischer
Other Expenses Budget
For the Year Ended December 31, 2002

Item	Amount
Travel	$
Meals	
Total	$

5. Using the schedule below, prepare a budgeted income statement for the year ended December 31, 2002.

Billick and Fischer
Budgeted Income Statement
For the Year Ended December 31, 2002

Revenues		$
Operating Costs:		
Professional Labor	$	
Overhead Support		
Other Expenses		
Operating Income		$

Part V

Miller and Tracey, attorneys, have been using a simplified costing system in which all professional labor costs are included in a single direct cost category—professional labor. All overhead costs are included in a single indirect cost pool—professional support—and are allocated to jobs using professional labor hours as the allocation base. Consider two clients: Ajax Industries, which required 50 hours of tax work; and Richard Stevens, who required 45 hours of litigation work. The firm has two partners who each earn a salary of $125,000 per year and five associates who each earn $70,000 per year. Each professional has 1,500 billable hours per year. The professional support costs of $410,000 consist of $280,000 of litigation support and $130,000 of secretarial support. Ajax's job required 10 hours of partner time and 40 hours of associate time. Stevens' job required 30 hours of partner time and 15 hours of associate time.

Instructions:

1. Complete the cost of the Ajax and Stevens jobs using a simplified costing system with one direct and one indirect cost pool.

	Ajax Industries	**Richard Stevens**
Professional Labor Cost:		
....	$	
....		$
Professional Support:		
....		
....		
Total..	$	$

Computations:

2. Compute the cost of the Ajax and Stevens jobs using an activity-based costing system with two direct cost categories—partner labor and associate labor—and two indirect cost categories—litigation support and secretarial support. Use partner labor dollars as the cost allocation base for litigation support and professional labor hours as the base for secretarial support.

	Ajax Industries	Richard Stevens
Professional Labor Cost:		
.... $		
....		$
Associate Labor Cost:		
....		
....		
Litigation Support:		
....		
....		
Secretarial Support:		
....		
....		
Total...	$_____	$_____

Computations:

CHAPTER 10 COST ANALYSIS FOR MANAGEMENT DECISION MAKING

Review Summary

1. **Absorption costing** assigns direct materials and direct labor costs and a share of both fixed and variable factory overhead costs to units of production. In **direct costing**, only direct materials, direct labor, and variable factory overhead are charged to the product, while fixed manufacturing costs are expensed totally in the period incurred.

   If the number of units produced differs from the number of units sold, reported net income under absorption costing will differ from reported net income under direct costing. This difference is caused by the elimination of fixed manufacturing expenses from inventories in direct costing. Generally, when production exceeds sales, absorption costing shows a higher profit than does direct costing, and when sales exceed production, the reverse occurs. Managers prefer income statements prepared on a direct costing basis because the variable cost of goods sold varies directly with sales volume, and the influence of production on profit is eliminated.

   The use of direct costing for financial reporting is not accepted by the American Institute of Certified Public Accountants, the Internal Revenue Service, the Securities and Exchange Commission, or the Financial Accounting Standards Board. The position of these groups generally is based on their opposition to excluding fixed costs from inventories. Companies using direct costing internally adjust to absorption costing when preparing income tax returns and when reporting externally.

2. **Segment reporting** provides data that can be used by management to evaluate the operations and profitability of individual divisions, product lines, sales territories, etc. **Segment profitability analysis** requires that all costs be classified as either **direct costs**, which can be traced to a specific segment, or **indirect costs**, which are common to all segments. The variable costs and direct fixed costs are subtracted from sales to obtain the **segment margin**, which measures the ability of the segment to recover both the assigned variable costs and direct fixed costs necessary to keep the company solvent. Segment profitability analysis is useful for making long-run decisions such as product pricing policies and changes in production capacities.

3. **Break-even analysis** indicates the point at which the company neither makes a profit nor suffers a loss. A **break-even chart** is a graphic analysis of the relationship of costs and sales to profit. **Cost-volume-profit analysis** is concerned with determining the optimal level and mix of output to be produced with available resources. The **contribution margin ratio** is determined by dividing the contribution margin (sales minus variable costs) by sales revenue. The **contribution margin per unit** is the difference between the sales price per unit and the variable costs per unit. Formulas for break-even computations follow:

$$\text{Break-even sales volume in dollars} = \frac{\text{Total fixed cost}}{1 - \dfrac{\text{Total variable costs}}{\text{Total sales}}}$$

$$\text{Break-even sales volume in units} = \frac{\text{Total fixed cost}}{\text{Sales price per unit} - \text{Variable cost per unit}}$$

4. Significant uses of break-even analysis include aiding in budgetary control, improving and balancing sales, analyzing the impact of volume changes, and analyzing the impact of sales price changes and changes in costs. The break-even chart is fundamentally a static analysis. The amount of fixed and variable costs, as well as the slope of the sales line, is meaningful only in a defined range of activity and must be redefined for activity outside the relevant range.

5. If management wishes to determine the amount of sales units or dollars needed to earn a certain income, known as the **target volume**, it may revise the break-even formula as follows:

$$\text{Target volume (dollars)} = \frac{\text{Total fixed costs} + \text{Net income}}{\text{Contribution margin ratio}}$$

If income taxes are present, the pre-tax income required to earn a certain net income must first be determined before the target volume can be computed. In a multi-product firm, a **weighted-average contribution margin** must be computed before the break-even sales volume or target volume can be determined.

6. The **margin of safety** indicates how much sales may decrease from a selected sales figure before the company will incur a loss and is computed as follows:

$$\text{Margin of safety} = \text{Sales} - \text{Break-even sales}$$

The margin of safety expressed as a percentage of sales is called the **margin of safety ratio** and is computed as follows:

$$\text{M/S ratio} = \frac{\text{Total sales} - \text{Break-even sales}}{\text{Total sales}}$$

Since the margin of safety is related directly to net income, the M/S ratio can be used to calculate net income as a percentage of sales:

$$\text{Net income percentage} = \text{Contribution margin ratio} \times \text{M/S ratio}$$

7. **Differential cost analyses** are studies that highlight the significant cost data of alternatives. Is it advantageous to sell a product at a special price? If there is excess capacity and the selling price per unit exceeds the variable costs per unit, the order should be accepted as long as it doesn't violate federal pricing legislation or alienate current customers. Another decision involves buying a part versus making it. If excess capacity exists, only the differential materials, labor, and overhead costs should be compared to the outside purchase price in deciding whether to make or buy.

8. Efficient control of all costs should include both the production costs and distribution costs. **Distribution costs** are costs incurred to sell and deliver the product. In allocating distribution costs to products and other cost objects, a reasonable basis for allocation, such as square inches of newspaper space for advertising costs, should be devised.

Part I

Instructions: Indicate your answer in the Answers column by writing a "T" for True or an "F" for False.

Answers

1. The absorption costing method charges the product with only the costs that vary directly with volume. .... _____

2. Under both absorption and direct costing, nonmanufacturing costs are charged against income in the period incurred........................... _____

3. Under absorption costing, fixed factory overhead expenses appear as an expense on each period's income statement. .... _____

4. If production exceeds sales, profits reported under direct costing will be less than profits reported under absorption costing.................... _____

5. Direct costing does not conform to generally accepted accounting principles for costing inventories.................................... _____

6. Indirect costs are excluded from the computation of the segment margin. . _____

7. In computing the break-even sales volume in units, the total fixed cost is divided by the contribution margin per unit. .... _____

8. In constructing a break-even chart, a variable cost line is drawn parallel to the X-axis. .... _____

9. The margin of safety ratio can be obtained by dividing net income as a percentage of sales by the contribution margin ratio. .... _____

10. A limitation of cost-volume-profit analysis is that it assumes that all factors except volume will remain constant for a period of time. .... _____

11. The margin of safety is computed by subtracting break-even sales from forecast sales.. _____

12. A study that highlights the significant cost data of alternatives is referred to as fixed cost analysis.. _____

13. To decide in favor of accepting an order at a special reduced price, there should be excess production capacity and the sales price per unit should exceed the variable cost per unit............................... _____

14. In deciding to make a part in its own plant or to buy it from a supplier, the relevant costs are the purchase price of the part and the manufacturer's fixed factory overhead. .... _____

15. In allocating advertising cost to products, the best basis to use is the amount of revenue that each product earned........................... _____

Part II

Instructions: In the Answers column, place the letter from the list below that identifies the term that best matches the statement. No letter should be used more than once.

a. Absorption costing
b. Break-even point
c. Sales mix
d. Variable costing
e. Contribution margin
f. Marginal income ratio
g. Distribution costs
h. Segment margin
i. Period costs
j. Margin of safety
k. Target volume
l. Cost-volume-profit analysis
m. Margin of safety ratio
n. Product costs
o. Differential cost analysis

Answers

_____ 1. This charges the product with only the costs that vary with volume.

_____ 2. These are costs that will be incurred whether or not the product is manufactured.

_____ 3. This charges the product with both fixed and variable expenses.

_____ 4. The amount of sales in units or dollars needed to cover costs and earn a certain profit.

_____ 5. The relative percentage of unit sales among the various products made by a firm.

_____ 6. The excess of segment revenue over direct costs assigned to the segment.

_____ 7. An analytical technique that uses the degrees of cost variability for measuring the effect of changes in volume on profits.

_____ 8. Where sales revenue is adequate to cover all costs to manufacture and sell the product but no profit is earned.

_____ 9. The difference between the sales revenue and the total variable expenses.

_____ 10. The amount by which sales can decrease before the company will suffer a loss.

_____ 11. Studies that highlight the significant cost data of alternatives.

_____ 12. These are costs incurred to sell and deliver the product.

_____ 13. A relationship computed by dividing the difference between the total sales and the break-even point sales by the total sales.

_____ 14. When inventory is sold these are recognized as expenses and matched with the related revenue.

_____ 15. It is the relationship between contribution margin and sales.

Name _____

Part III

Instructions: In the Answers column, place the letter of the choice that most correctly completes each item.

Answers

_____ 1. To institute a direct costing system, it is necessary to know:
   a. The variable and fixed components of all costs related to production
   b. The controllable and noncontrollable components of all costs related to production
   c. Standard production rates and times for all elements of production
   d. The contribution margin and break-even point for all goods in production

_____ 2. The difference in operating income computed using absorption costing and operating income computed using direct costing, related to manufacturing costs, occurs because:
   a. Absorption costing considers all costs in the determination of operating income, whereas direct costing considers only direct costs
   b. Absorption costing inventories all direct costs, but direct costing considers direct costs to be period costs
   c. Absorption costing inventories all fixed costs for the period in ending finished goods inventory, but direct costing expenses all fixed costs
   d. Absorption costing allocates fixed costs between cost of goods sold and inventories, while direct costing considers all fixed costs to be period costs

_____ 3. If the ending inventory decreases with respect to the beginning inventory in terms of units, in comparing operating income using direct costing vs. absorption costing:
   a. There will be no difference in operating income
   b. Operating income computed using direct costing will be higher
   c. The difference in operating income cannot be determined from the information given
   d. Operating income computed using direct costing will be lower

_____ 4. A company has operating income of $50,000 using direct costing for a given period. Beginning and ending inventories for that period were 18,000 units and 13,000 units, respectively. If the fixed factory overhead application rate is $1 per unit, the operating income using absorption costing is:
   a. $45,000
   b. $55,000
   c. $50,000
   d. not determinable from the information given

_____ 5. Solar Company sells Product Q at $8 per unit. In 2002, fixed cost is expected to be $200,000 and variable cost is estimated at $4 per unit. The units of Q that Solar must sell to generate operating income of $40,000 are:
   a. 50,000   c. 60,000
   b. 100,000   d. 120,000

6. If the fixed cost for a product increases and the variable cost (as a percentage of sales dollars) increases, what will be the effect on the contribution margin ratio and the break-even point, respectively?

	Contribution Margin Ratio	Break-Even Point
a.	Decreased	Increased
b.	Increased	Decreased
c.	Decreased	Decreased
d.	Increased	Increased

7. To obtain the target volume stated in dollars of sales, divide the total fixed cost plus desired net income by:
   a. Variable cost per unit
   b. (Sales price per unit – variable cost per unit) ÷ sales price per unit
   c. Fixed cost per unit
   d. Variable cost per unit ÷ sales price per unit

8. The manufacturing capacity of Paul Company's facilities is 30,000 units of a product a year. A summary of operating results for the year ended December 31, 2002, follows:

Sales (18,000 units @ $100 per unit)............................	$1,800,000
Variable manufacturing and selling costs	990,000
Contribution margin	810,000
Fixed costs	495,000
Operating income	$ 315,000

A foreign distributor has offered to buy 15,000 units at $90 per unit during 2003. Assume that all of Paul's costs would be at the same levels and rates in 2003 as in 2002. If Paul accepted this offer and rejected some business from regular customers so as not to exceed capacity, what would be the total operating income for 2003?
   a. $390,000   c. $840,000
   b. $705,000   d. $855,000

9. Mozart Company sells Product A at a selling price of $21 per unit. Mozart's cost per unit based on the full capacity of 200,000 units follows:

Direct materials	$ 4
Direct labor...	5
Overhead (two-thirds of which is fixed)............................	6
	$15

A special order offering to buy 20,000 units was received from a foreign distributor. The only selling costs that would be incurred on this order are $3 per unit for shipping. Mozart has sufficient existing capacity to manufacture the additional units. In negotiating a price for the special order, Mozart should consider that the minimum selling price per unit should exceed:
   a. $14   c. $16
   b. $15   d. $18

____ **10.** Toni Company temporarily has unused production capacity. The idle plant facilities can be used to manufacture a low-margin item. This low-margin item should be produced if it can be sold for more than its:
   a. Fixed cost
   b. Variable manufacturing cost
   c. Variable manufacturing and marketing costs
   d. Variable marketing cost

Part IV

Flashpoint Manufacturing Company has determined the cost of manufacturing a unit of product to be as follows, based on normal production of 50,000 units per year:

Direct materials	$10
Direct labor..	8
Variable factory overhead..............................	6
	$24
Fixed factory overhead...................................	6
	$30

Operating statistics for the months of July and August are as follows:

	July	August
Units produced...	6,000	4,000
Units sold...	4,000	6,000
Selling and administrative expenses..............	$25,000	$25,000

The selling price is $40 per unit. There were no inventories on July 1, and there is no work in process at August 31.

Instructions: Complete the comparative income statements on the next page for July and August for Flashpoint under:

1. absorption costing
2. direct costing

Flashpoint Manufacturing Company
Income Statement
For the Month Ended July 31, 2002

	Absorption Costing	Direct Costing
Sales	$	$
Cost of goods sold..		_____
Underapplied/overapplied factory overhead*......................	_____	
Gross margin	$	
Contribution margin..		$
Less:		
Fixed factory overhead...................................		
Selling and administrative expenses..........................	_____	_____
Net income (loss)	$_____	$_____

*Calculation of overapplied factory overhead:

Fixed factory overhead per year..		$_____
Fixed factory overhead per month		$_____
Fixed factory overhead applied to production		$
Fixed overhead per month..		_____
Fixed factory overhead overapplied......................................		$_____

Flashpoint Manufacturing Company
Income Statement
For the Month Ended August 31, 2002

	Absorption Costing	Direct Costing
Sales	$	$
Cost of goods sold..		_____
Underapplied/overapplied factory overhead**....................	_____	
Gross margin	$	
Contribution margin..		$
Less:		
Fixed factory overhead...................................		
Selling and administrative expenses..........................	_____	_____
Net income (loss)	$_____	$_____

**Calculation of underapplied factory overhead:

Fixed factory overhead applied to production		$
Fixed factory overhead per month		_____
Fixed factory overhead underapplied......................................		$_____

Part V

The following data of Stratton Co. are given for May:

Normal capacity.........................	1,600 units for the month
Fixed cost.................................	$80,000 per month
Variable cost.............................	$60 per unit
Sales price	$150 per unit

Instructions:

1. Determine the break-even point in dollars (round to the nearest whole dollar).

2. Determine the break-even point in units (round to the nearest whole unit).

3. When operating at normal plant capacity, compute the margin of safety in units and the margin of safety ratio (round to the nearest whole unit and whole percent).

4. Prepare a break-even chart, using the form below. Label and identify each element of the chart.

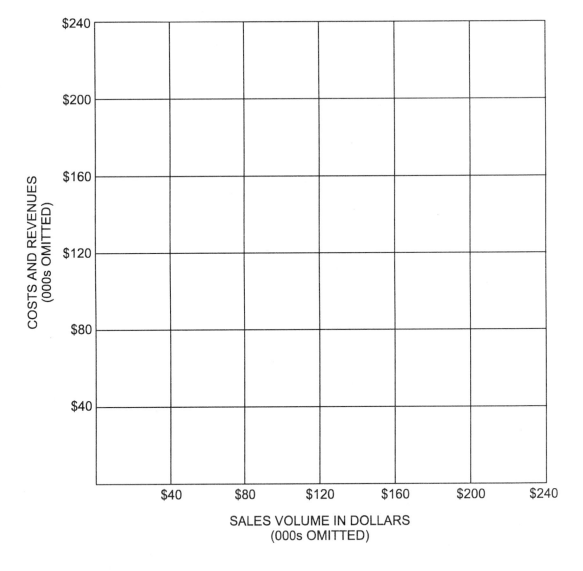

5. Determine the target volume in units needed to earn an after-tax income of $10,000 per month, assuming a tax rate of 30%.

Name _____

Part VI

Although Bliss Company has the capacity to produce 10,000 units per month, current plans call for monthly production and sales of only 8,000 units at $15 each. Costs per unit at the 8,000 unit level follow:

Direct materials	$ 4.00
Direct labor	2.50
Variable factory overhead	2.00
Fixed factory overhead	1.75
Variable marketing expense	.50
Fixed administrative expense	1.25
	$12.00

Instructions:

1. Determine whether the company should accept a special order for 1,000 units @ $8.00 per unit.

2. Determine the maximum unit price that the company should be willing to pay an outside supplier to manufacture 10,000 units of this product, assuming that $2,500 of fixed factory overhead would not be incurred if the product were made outside.

CHAPTER 1 SOLUTIONS

Part I

1. T	**6.** T	**11.** F
2. F	**7.** F	**12.** T
3. T	**8.** T	**13.** F
4. T	**9.** T	**14.** F
5. T	**10.** F	**15.** T

Part II

1. p	**8.** l	**15.** r
2. h	**9.** b	**16.** e
3. q	**10.** f	**17.** n
4. a	**11.** s	**18.** i
5. j	**12.** m	**19.** k
6. d	**13.** c	**20.** g
7. t	**14.** o	

Part III

1. (d) When direct materials are transferred to the factory for use in production, Work in Process is debited and Materials are credited.

2. (d) Standard costs are predetermined costs for direct materials, direct labor, and factory overhead that are established by using information accumulated from past experience and from scientific research. Budgets should be based on standard costs.

3. (a) Only manufacturing costs are inventoriable.

4. (d) Process costing accumulates costs by production process or department. It is used when units are not separately distinguishable from one another during one or more manufacturing processes.

5. (b) Beverage production usually consists of manufacturing "long runs" of homogeneous products for which process costing is used. The other three industries would utilize job order costing.

6. (c) Plant insurance is a factory overhead cost because it is a manufacturing cost that cannot be identified with specific jobs.

7. (b) When items in Work in Process are completed and transferred to the finished goods storeroom, Finished Goods is debited and Work in Process is credited.

8. (c) The cost of goods sold is determined as follows:

Beginning finished goods inventory	$ 25,000
Add cost of goods manufactured	500,000
Goods available for sale	$525,000
Less ending finished goods inventory	50,000
Cost of goods sold	$475,000

Cost of goods sold ($475,000) plus gross profit ($150,000) equals sales of $625,000.

9. (c) Beginning finished goods inventory .... $ 40,000
         Cost of goods manufactured..   260,000
         Goods available for sale $300,000
         Less: Ending finished goods inventory................................   32,000
         Cost of goods sold $268,000

         Sales... $323,000
         Cost of goods sold   268,000
         Gross profit.. $ 55,000

Note: The beginning and ending inventories of work in process have no significance in this
         calculation because they would have been used in determining the cost of goods
         manufactured which was given.

10. (c) Answers (a), (b), and (d) are all uses of unit costs for making marketing decisions.

Part IV

	Indirect Materials	Indirect Labor	Other Indirect Manufacturing Costs	Selling and Administrative Expenses
1.				✓
2.			✓	
3.	✓			
4.		✓		
5.				✓
6.				✓
7.				✓
8.				✓
9.			✓	
10.			✓	
11.			✓	
12.				✓
13.	✓			
14.	✓			
15.				✓
16.			✓	
17.				✓
18.				✓
19.		✓		
20.		✓		

Part V

	Debit	Credit
1.	d	j
2.	j	d
3.	j	i
4.	g, f	d
5.	e	o
6.	o	i
7.	f, g, h	e
8.	f, h	k
9.	l	i
10.	f	l
11.	f, h	j
12.	g	f
13.	a	g
14.	b, m	a, n

Part VI

Harvey Company
Statement of Cost of Goods Manufactured
For the Year Ended December 31, 2001

Direct materials:		
Inventory, January 1	$15,000	
Purchases	22,000	
Total cost of available materials	$37,000	
Less inventory, December 31	10,000	
Cost of materials used	$27,000	
Less indirect materials used	3,000	
Cost of direct materials used in production		$24,000
Direct labor		30,000
Factory overhead:		
Indirect materials	$ 3,000	
Indirect labor	8,000	
Other factory overhead	7,500	
Total factory overhead		18,500
Total manufacturing cost		$72,500
Add work-in-process inventory, January 1		25,000
Total		$97,500
Less work-in-process inventory, December 31		20,000
Cost of goods manufactured		$77,500

CHAPTER 2 SOLUTIONS

Part I

1. T	6. T	11. T
2. T	7. T	12. T
3. F	8. T	13. T
4. T	9. F	14. F
5. F	10. T	15. T

Part II

1. o	8. a	15. g
2. s	9. b	16. l
3. e	10. c	17. k
4. p	11. q	18. i
5. r	12. n	19. j
6. d	13. f	20. h
7. t	14. m	

Part III

1. (b) If normal spoilage is caused by exacting specifications, difficult processing, or other unusual and unexpected factors, the spoilage cost should be charged to that order.

2. (d) Since under FIFO the earliest goods purchased are the first goods considered to be sold, the most recently purchased merchandise would be assignable to inventory.

3. (c) Choices (a), (b), and (d) are all valid reasons in favor of using the LIFO method. Statement (c), however, is more typical of the FIFO method, in that the earliest goods purchased by a business are usually the first ones sold.

4. (a) If the inventory cost on the balance sheet was higher using FIFO than LIFO, the most recent purchases (which would appear on the balance sheet under FIFO) were more expensive than the earlier purchases (which would appear on the balance sheet using LIFO).

5. (c) $\sqrt{\dfrac{2CN}{K}} = \sqrt{\dfrac{2 \times 50{,}000 \times \$6.25}{\$10}} = 250$

6. (a)
   $$\begin{aligned} 175 \text{ units} \times 8 \text{ days} &= 1{,}400 \\ \text{safety stock} & +\underline{1{,}000} \\ & \underline{2{,}400} \end{aligned}$$

7. (c) In determining EOQ, only the variable ordering costs, such as preparing the purchase order, handling the incoming shipment, and preparing the receiving report, should be considered.

8. (d) If the additional costs for correcting the imperfections in defective units are incurred on orders that the company regularly processes, they are charged to factory overhead.

9. (a) The EOQ is that point where carrying costs equal order costs. If a quantity smaller than the EOQ is ordered, ordering costs will exceed carrying costs.

10. (c) If safety stocks are ignored, the only factor relevant for determining the order point would be the anticipated demand during the lead time.

Part IV

1. $EOQ = \sqrt{\dfrac{2CN}{K}} = \sqrt{\dfrac{2 \times \$20 \times 20,000}{\$5}} = \sqrt{\dfrac{\$800,000}{\$5}} = \sqrt{160,000} = 400 \text{ units}$

2.

(1) Order Size	(2) Number of Orders	(3) Total Order Cost	(4) Average Inventory	(5) Total Carrying Cost	(6) Total Order & Carrying Costs
100	200	$4,000	50	$ 250	$4,250
200	100	2,000	100	500	2,500
300	67	1,340	150	750	2,090
400	50	1,000	200	1,000	2,000
500	40	800	250	1,250	2,050
600	34	680	300	1,500	2,180
700	29	580	350	1,750	2,330
800	25	500	400	2,000	2,500

3. Order point = (Daily usage × Lead time) + Safety stock
    = [(20,000 ÷ 250) × 5] + 200
    = <u>600</u> units

Part V

1. First-in, first-out costing

Date	Received Quantity	Received Unit Price	Received Amount	Issued Quantity	Issued Unit Price	Issued Amount	Balance Quantity	Balance Unit Price	Balance Amount	
Mar. 2	200	$ 9	$1,800				200	$ 9	$1,800	
8	60	10	600				60	10	600	$2,400
18				100	$ 9	$900	100	9	900	
							60	10	600	1,500
24	240	12	2,880				240	12	2,880	4,380
31				100	9	900				
				60	10	600				
				40	12	480	200	12	2,400	

Cost of materials consumed........................ $2,880

Cost assigned to inventory $2,400

2. Last-in, first-out costing

Date	Received			Issued			Balance		
	Quantity	Unit Price	Amount	Quantity	Unit Price	Amount	Quantity	Unit Price	Amount
Mar. 2	200	$ 9	$1,800				200	$ 9	$1,800
8	60	10	600				60	10	600 $2,400
18				60	$10	$ 600			
				40	9	360	160	9	1,400
24	240	12	2,880				240	12	2,880 4,320
31				200	12	2,400	160	9	1,440
							40	12	480 1,920

Cost of materials consumed........................ $3,360

Cost assigned to inventory $1,920

3. Moving average method

Date	Received			Issued			Balance		
	Quantity	Unit Price	Amount	Quantity	Unit Price	Amount	Quantity	Unit Price	Amount
Mar. 2	200	$ 9	$1,800				200	$ 9.00	$1,800
8	60	10	600				260	9.23	2,400
18				100	$ 9.23	$ 923	160	9.23	1,477
24	240	12	2,880				400	10.89	4,357
31				200	10.89	2,178	200	10.89	2,179

Cost of materials consumed........................ $3,101

Cost assigned to inventory $2,179

Part VI

1. No.	Account	Debit	Credit
a.	Materials	125,500	
	Accounts Payable		125,500
b.	Work in Process	90,900	
	Materials		90,900
c.	Materials	3,750	
	Work in Process		3,750
d.	Factory Overhead (Indirect Materials)	4,850	
	Materials		4,850
e.	Materials	720	
	Factory Overhead (Indirect Materials)		720
f.	Accounts Payable	98,250	
	Cash		98,250
g.	Factory Overhead (Inventory Short and Over)	250	
	Materials		250

2.

Cash			
Bal. 100,000	(f)	98,250
1,750		

Materials			
Bal.	75,000		
(a)	125,500	(b)	90,900
(c)	3,750	(d)	4,850
(e)	720	(g)	250
	204,970		96,000
	108,970		

Work in Process			
(b)	90,900	(c)	3,750
87,150			

Accounts Payable			
(f)	98,250	(a)	125,500
		27,250	

Factory Overhead			
(d)	4,850	(e)	720
(g)	250		
	4,380		

3. The balance of the materials account on September 30 is $108,970.

Part VII

1.		Cash...	200	
		Work in Process—Job AC101		200
2.	**a.**	Scrap Materials..	2,000	
		Factory Overhead		2,000
	b.	Accounts Receivable	2,000	
		Scrap Materials..		2,000
3.		Spoiled Goods Inventory	150	
		Work in Process—Job AC102		150
4.		Factory Overhead (Rework Costs)...........................	600	
		Materials..		300
		Payroll..		200
		Factory Overhead		100

Part VIII (Appendix)

a.	Raw and In-Process..	160,000	
	Accounts Payable..		160,000
b.	No Entry		
c.	Conversion Costs..	20,000	
	Payroll		20,000
d.	Conversion Costs..	120,000	
	Various Credits...		120,000
e.	Cost of Goods Sold	300,000	
	Raw and In-Process		160,000
	Conversion Costs...		140,000

CHAPTER 3 SOLUTIONS

Part I

1. F	6. F	11. F
2. T	7. T	12. T
3. T	8. F	13. F
4. T	9. T	14. F
5. T	10. T	15. T

Part II

1. d	8. c	15. r
2. i	9. q	16. o
3. h	10. s	17. j
4. p	11. b	18. n
5. m	12. e	19. k
6. t	13. g	20. l
7. a	14. f	

Part III

1. (d) Before the daily time tickets go to the payroll department, the total time reported on each time ticket is compared with the total hours on each employee's clock card. If any difference exists, an adjustment is made after having identified the reasons for the difference.

2. (c) The clock card (or time card) is needed to provide evidence of the employee's presence in the plant from the time of entry to departure.

3. (d) Fringe costs form a substantial element of labor cost and include such items as the employer portion of the FICA tax, holiday pay, overtime premium pay, and pension costs.

4. (c) A piece-rate plan is an incentive wage plan which bases earnings on the employee's quantity of production.

5. (b) Payroll taxes are treated as an indirect manufacturing cost and are debited to Factory Overhead when the payroll is recorded.

6. (d) In determining whether the overtime premium should be charged to a specific job or spread over all jobs via the factory overhead rate, the key consideration is whether the job was worked on during the overtime period because it was a rush order or merely as a result of random scheduling.

7. (d) $\dfrac{\$800 \times 4 \text{ weeks}}{48 \text{ weeks}} = \$66.67$

8. (b) To spread the bonus cost over production throughout the year via the predetermined factory overhead rate, the weekly entry would include a debit to Factory Overhead Control for the ratable portion of the bonus pay.

9. (c) Theoretically the employer's share of the payroll taxes should be charged to direct labor and indirect labor. However, due to the additional expense and time required for such allocation, all factory payroll taxes are usually charged to Factory Overhead.

10. (b) In a highly automated manufacturing environment there usually would be significant direct materials to be converted to finished products, substantial indirect laborers, such as engineers, programmers, and repair and maintenance personnel, and large amounts of depreciation on the costly equipment, but there would be few direct laborers needed to produce the product.

Part IV

Day	Earnings at $10 per Hour	Earnings at $2.50 per Piece	Make-up Guarantee	Daily Earnings	Labor Cost per Unit
Monday	$80	$ 75	$ 5	$ 80	$2.67
Tuesday	$80	80	–	80	2.50
Wednesday	$80	115	–	115	2.50
Thursday	$80	70	10	80	2.86
Friday	$80	85	–	85	2.50

Part V

1.

	Dillon	Smith	Spikes	Warrick	Total
Hours worked..................		40	46	40	
Piecework........................	780				
Rate (hourly/piece)	$.50	$7.00	$8.80	$12.20	
Direct labor	$390.00		$404.80		$794.80
Indirect labor..................		$280.00		$488.00	$768.00
Overtime premium..........			26.40		26.40
Gross pay........................	$390.00	$280.00	$431.20	$488.00	$1,589.20
Income tax (15%)	$ 58.50	$ 42.00	$ 64.68	$ 73.20	$ 238.38
FICA tax (8%)	31.20	22.40	34.50	39.04	127.14
Health insurance (3%)	11.70	8.40	12.94	14.64	47.68
Total deductions.............	$101.40	$ 72.80	$112.12	$126.88	$ 413.20
Net pay	$288.60	$207.20	$319.08	$361.12	$1,176.00

2. **(a)** Payroll 1,589.20

            FICA Tax Payable 127.14

            Employees Income Tax Payable 238.38

            Health Insurance Premiums Payable 47.68

            Wages Payable 1,176.00

   (b) Wages Payable 1,176.00

            Cash 1,176.00

   (c) Work in Process 794.80

       Factory Overhead* 794.40

            Payroll 1,589.20

   (d) Factory Overhead 206.60

            FICA Tax Payable 127.14

            Federal Unemployment Tax Payable** 15.89

            State Unemployment Tax Payable*** 63.57

  * $768 + $26.40

  ** Federal unemployment tax = $1,589.20 × 1% = $15.89

*** State unemployment tax = $1,589.20 × 4% = $63.57

Part VI

1. Work in Process 1,100

     Payroll   1,100

2. Work in Process 1,000

   Factory Overhead 100

     Payroll   1,100

Part VII

Work in Process 2,200.00

Factory Overhead (Bonus)* 200.00

Factory Overhead (Vacation)** 200.00

Factory Overhead (Holiday Pay)*** 92.31

   Payroll 2,200.00

   Bonus Liability 200.00

   Vacation Pay Liability 200.00

   Holiday Pay Liability 92.31

  * $2,200 ÷ 11 months

 ** $2,200 ÷ 11 months

*** $2,200 × 12 months = $26,400 ÷ 52 weeks = $507.69 weekly pay

   $507.69 × 2 weeks = $1,015.38 holiday pay ÷ 11 months = $92.31

CHAPTER 4 SOLUTIONS

Part I

1. T	6. T	11. F
2. F	7. T	12. F
3. F	8. T	13. T
4. T	9. T	14. T
5. F	10. F	15. F

Part II

1. f	8. t	15. m
2. s	9. e	16. n
3. h	10. d	17. i
4. l	11. a	18. q
5. g	12. c	19. k
6. b	13. r	20. j
7. o	14. p	

Part III

1. (d) When the overhead applied to jobs or products during the period is more than the actual overhead incurred, overhead is said to be overapplied.

2. (b) The fixed cost per unit would increase because the same dollar amount of fixed cost is being spread over a smaller number of units. The per unit variable cost is unchanged because as fewer units are produced, total variable cost decreases.

3. (a) There should be a high degree of correlation between the base being used and the type of overhead cost incurred. Answers (b), (c), and (d) are examples of bases that frequently are used.

4. (a) If factory overhead costs are mostly variable, changes in the level of production should have little effect on the amount of overhead cost applied to products.

5. (a) The direct labor hours method is considered the most accurate method of applying overhead when the wage rates of the direct laborers vary greatly and overhead cost is more a function of the number of labor hours worked, rather than the cost of the labor that does the work.

6. (d) Activity-based costing is the method that considers non-volume-related activities that create overhead costs, such as machine setups and design changes, as well as volume-related activities, such as labor hours and machine hours.

7. (d) A service department renders a service that contributes in an indirect manner to the manufacture of the product, but that does not itself change the shape, form, or nature of the material that is converted into the finished product.

8. (b) All of the other departments listed are production departments.

9. (a) To charge each department with its fair share of an expense, a base using some factor common to all departments must be found. Therefore, the number of employees would be a good base to use for allocating the cost of operating the human resources department.

10. (a) The direct distribution method allocates service department costs to production departments only, thus being the least precise method of distribution.

Part IV

	Direct Labor Hours	Electricity Expense
High volume	720	$38,000
Low volume	320	22,000
Difference	400	$16,000

Variable cost per direct labor hour: $16,000 ÷ 400 = $40

Fixed cost:	Cost at low volume	$22,000
	Variable cost (320 × $40)	12,800
	Fixed cost	$ 9,200

OR

Fixed cost:	Cost at high volume	$38,000
	Variable cost (720 × $40)	28,800
	Fixed cost	$ 9,200

Part V

	Total	Preparation	Mixing	Packaging	Utilities	Maintenance	Materials Handling	Factory Office
		Production Departments			**Service Departments**			
Distribution of service departments:								
Utilities:								
70% metered hours		(30%) 1,512[a]	(36%) 1,814	(14%) 706		(10%) 504	(6%) 302	(4%) 202
30% sq. footage		(36%) 778	(26%) 562	(24%) 518		(4%) 86	(2%) 43	(8%) 173[b]
					(5,040)			
					(2,160)			
					$7,200			
Maintenance		(50%) 2,395	(25%) 1,198	(10%) 479		$4,790[c]	(10%) 479	(5%) 239
						$(4,790)		
Materials handling		(45%) 1,664	(35%) 1,295	(20%) 740			$3,699[d]	$3,189[e]
							$(3,699)	
Factory office		(50%) 1,594	(40%) 1,276	(10%) 319				$(3,189)
	$35,500	$13,943[f]	$11,845[g]	$9,712[h]				
Bases:								
Pounds handled		500,000	300,000					
Direct labor costs				$10,000				
Rates		$.0279 per pound handled	$.0395 per pound handled	97.12% of direct labor cost				

$7,200 × .70 = $5,040

$7,200 × .30 = $2,160

[a] 1,500 ÷ 5,000 × $5,040 = $1,512

[b] 4,000 ÷ 50,000 × $2,160 = $173

[c] $4,200 + $504 + $86 = $4,790

[d] $2,875 + $302 + $43 + $479 = $3,699

[e] $2,575 + $202 + $173 + $239 = $3,189

[f] $6,000 + $1,512 + $778 + $2,395 + $1,664 + $1,594 = $13,943

[g] $5,700 + $1,814 + $562 + $1,198 + $1,295 + $1,276 = $11,845

[h] $6,950 + $706 + $518 + $479 + $740 + $319 = $9,712

Part VI

Cost of Job H202:

Direct materials	$ 5,000
Direct labor	2,000
Factory overhead:	
Direct labor usage (400 hrs. × $20/hr.)	8,000
Machine usage (200 hrs. × $40/hr.)	8,000
Machine setups (2 setups × $1,000/setup)	2,000
Design changes (1 design change × $2,000/change)	2,000
Total cost	$27,000

CHAPTER 5 SOLUTIONS

Part I

1. T	6. F	11. F
2. F	7. T	12. T
3. T	8. F	13. T
4. F	9. T	14. F
5. T	10. T	15. F

Part II

1. j	5. i	8. g
2. c	6. b	9. f
3. a	7. h	10. d
4. e		

Part III

1. (d) All of the statements in (a) through (c) are features of process costing.

2. (b) The cost per job would appear on a job order cost sheet. Answers (a), (c), and (d) would all appear on a cost of production report.

3. (b) The dollar amount of production cost included in the ending work-in-process inventory is determined by multiplying the average unit costs by the percentage of completion of the ending work-in-process inventory (60%).

4. (c) Proof (figures assumed):

	Actual	As computed incorrectly	
Units completed during period............................	20,000	20,000	
Equivalent units in ending work in process........	1,000	2,000	
Total equivalent units	21,000	22,000	(O)
Production cost..	$462,000	$462,000	
Unit cost (production cost ÷ total equivalent units)...	$22.00	$21.00	(U)
Cost of goods completed:			
20,000 units × $22 unit cost............................	$440,000		
20,000 units × $21 unit cost............................		$420,000	(U)

5. (c) Unit output for month:

Finished during month	30,000
Equivalent units in ending work in process (12,000 units, 60% completed)......................................	7,200
	37,200

6. (d)

Units completed during month...	30,000
Less units in process, beginning of month...........................	(10,000)
Units started and completed during month..........................	20,000
Units in process, end of month..	12,000
Units started during month..	32,000

7. (b) It is also important to remember that costs transferred in are not part of the unit cost computation for the department to which they were transferred.

8. (a) An equivalent unit of material or conversion cost is equal to the amount of material or conversion cost necessary to complete one unit of production.

9. (b) Equivalent units of production applies only to process costing because in job order costing, costs are assigned directly to jobs; therefore, the concept of equivalent production isn't necessary.

10. (b) In computing the unit cost using average costing, the cost of the beginning work-in-process inventory is added to the current period costs and the total is divided by the equivalent units of production.

Part IV

	Debit	**Credit**
1.	Materials	Accounts Payable
2.	Work in Process—Department A Work in Process—Department B Factory Overhead	Materials
3.	Work in Process—Department A Work in Process—Department B Factory Overhead	Payroll
4.	Factory Overhead	Various Credits
5.	Factory Overhead—Department A Factory Overhead—Department B	Factory Overhead
6.	Work in Process—Department A Work in Process—Department B	Factory Overhead—Department A Factory Overhead—Department B
7.	Work in Process—Department B	Work in Process—Department A
8.	Finished Goods	Work in Process—Department B
9.	Cost of Goods Sold	Finished Goods

Part V

Salsa Manufacturing Company
Cost of Production Summary
For the Month Ended June 30, 2001

Cost of work in process, beginning of month:

Materials	$ 3,000	
Labor..	1,500	
Factory overhead	500	$ 5,000
Cost of production for month:		
Materials	$50,000	
Labor..	30,000	
Factory overhead	20,000	100,000
Total costs to be accounted for		$105,000

Unit output for month:

Finished during month...	18,000
Equivalent units of work in process, end of month	
(4,000 units, one-half completed).....................................	2,000
Total equivalent production	20,000

Unit cost for month:

Materials ($53,000 ÷ 20,000)...	$2.650
Labor ($31,500 ÷ 20,000)...	1.575
Factory overhead ($20,500 ÷ 20,000)...............................	1.025
Total..	$5.250

Inventory costs:

Cost of goods finished during month (18,000 × $5.25).......		$ 94,500
Cost of work in process, end of month:		
Materials (4,000 × 1/2 × $2.65).....................................	$5,300	
Labor (4,000 × 1/2 × $1.575)...	3,150	
Factory overhead (4,000 × 1/2 × $1.025)	2,050	10,500
Total production costs accounted for....................................		$105,000

Part VI

Falmouth Products
Cost of Production Summary—Machining
For the Month Ended May 31, 2001

Cost of work in process, beginning of month:

Materials	$ 4,000	
Labor	3,000	
Factory overhead	2,000	$ 9,000

Cost of production for month:

Materials	$68,000	
Labor	51,000	
Factory overhead	34,000	153,000
Total costs to be accounted for		$162,000

Unit output for month:

Finished and transferred to Assembly during month	5,000
Equivalent units of work in process, end of month (2,000, 1/2 completed)	1,000
Total equivalent production	6,000

Unit cost for month:

Materials ($72,000 ÷ 6,000)	$12
Labor ($54,000 ÷ 6,000)	9
Factory overhead ($36,000 ÷ 6,000)	6
Total	$27

Inventory costs:

Cost of goods finished and transferred to Assembly during month (5,000 × $27)		$135,000

Cost of work in process, end of month:

Materials (2,000 × 1/2 × $12)	$12,000	
Labor (2,000 × 1/2 × $9)	9,000	
Factory overhead (2,000 × 1/2 × $6)	6,000	27,000
Total production costs accounted for		$162,000

Falmouth Products
Cost of Production Summary—Assembly
For the Month Ended May 31, 2001

Cost of work in process, beginning of month:
Cost in Machining $27,000
Cost in Assembly:
   Materials... $800
   Labor.. 400
   Factory overhead.. 600   1,800 $ 28,800
Cost of goods received from Machining during month.......... 135,000
Cost of production for month:
   Materials $44,000
   Labor... 22,000
   Factory overhead 33,000   99,000
Total cost to be accounted for................................... $262,800

Unit output for month:
Finished and transferred to stockroom during month.......... 4,000
Equivalent units of work in process, end of month
   (2,000 units, 1/2 completed) 1,000
   Total equivalent production 5,000

Unit cost for month:
Materials ($44,800 ÷ 5,000)...................................... $ 8.96
Labor ($22,400 ÷ 5,000)... 4.48
Factory overhead ($33,600 ÷ 5,000).......................... 6.72
   Total $20.16

Inventory costs:
Cost of goods finished and transferred to stockroom
   during month:
Cost in Machining (4,000 × $27)................................ $108,000
Cost in Assembly (4,000 × $20.16) 80,640 $188,640
Cost of work in process, end of month:
Cost in Machining (2,000 × $27)................................ $ 54,000
Cost in Assembly:
   Materials (2,000 × 1/2 × $8.96)...................... $8,960
   Labor (2,000 × 1/2 × $4.48).......................... 4,480
   Factory overhead (2,000 × 1/2 × $6.72) 6,720   20,160   74,160
Total production costs accounted for........................... $262,800

CHAPTER 6
SOLUTIONS

Part I

1. T	**6.** T	**11.** F
2. T	**7.** F	**12.** T
3. F	**8.** T	**13.** T
4. T	**9.** F	**14.** T
5. F	**10.** T	**15.** F

Part II

1. i	**6.** m	**10.** c
2. a	**7.** b	**11.** d
3. j	**8.** k	**12.** l
4. e	**9.** g	**13.** f
5. h		

Part III

1. (a) The equivalent unit computation would include only the marketable units transferred out plus the work done on the units still in process at the end of the period.

2. (d) The cost of normal shrinkage and scrap is a product cost that attaches to the inventory rather than a period cost that is expensed when it occurs.

3. (b)
Units completed and transferred......................................	90,000
Ending work in process with 40% materials.....................	20,000
	110,000

4. (c) Unit output—Materials:
Beginning work in process	50,000
Transferred in......................................	200,000
Total	250,000
Less ending work in process...............	40,000
Finished and transferred out	210,000
Ending work in process (40,000 × 100%).............................	40,000
	250,000 units equivalent production

Unit output—Conversion Costs:
Transferred out....................................	210,000
Ending work in process (40,000 × 20%)...............................	8,000
	218,000 units equivalent production

5. (a) Under the FIFO method, the degree of completion of the beginning work in process must be stated in order to compute completed unit costs; average costing does not require the degree of completion of the beginning work in process.

6. (c) Equivalent units of production under FIFO = percent of work required to complete beginning inventory + units started and completed during period + percent of work performed on ending inventory.

7. (b) Since the cost of the beginning inventory is kept separate from the cost of the goods started and completed during the period under FIFO but not under average costing, the cost of goods manufactured would be the same under both methods when there is no beginning inventory.

8. (a) All manufacturing costs (materials, labor, and overhead) should be allocable as joint costs.

9. (a) Joint costs should be allocated in a manner that assigns a proportionate amount of the total cost to each product by means of a quantitative basis such as the market or sales value method, the quantitative or physical unit method, the average unit cost method, or the weighted average method.

10. (b) Gasoline: $\dfrac{\$9,000 - \$3,600}{\$15,000 - \$6,000} \times \$6,600 = \$3,960$

          Kerosene: $\dfrac{\$6,000 - \$2,400}{\$15,000 - \$6,000} \times \$6,600 = \$2,640$

Part IV

Meridian Manufacturing, Inc.
Cost of Production Summary—Assembly
For the Month of June 2002

Cost of work in process, beginning of month:			
Cost in Machining			$ 25,000
Cost in Assembly:			
Materials	–0–		
Labor	$2,720		
Factory overhead	1,360	4,080	$ 29,080
Cost of goods received from Machining during month			225,000
Cost of production for month:			
Materials		$ 10,000	
Labor		25,000	
Factory overhead		12,500	47,500
Total costs to be accounted for			$301,580
Unit output for month:			
Materials:			
Finished and transferred to Painting during month			38,000
Equivalent units of work in process, end of month			–0–
Finished and on hand			2,000
Total equivalent production			40,000
Labor and factory overhead:			
Finished and transferred to Painting during month			38,000
Equivalent units of work in process, end of month			
(10,000 units, one-half completed)			5,000
Finished and on hand			2,000
Total equivalent production			45,000

Unit cost for month:
    Materials ($10,000 ÷ 40,000)... $ .250
    Labor ($27,720 ÷ 45,000)...   .616
    Factory overhead ($13,860 ÷ 45,000)...............................   .308
       Total... $1.174

Inventory costs:
    Cost of goods finished and transferred to Painting during
      month:
    Cost in Machining (38,000 × $5.00*)........................... $190,000
    Cost in Assembly (38,000 × $1.174)............................   44,612 $234,612
Cost of work in process, end of month:
    Finished and on hand:
    Cost in Machining (2,000 × $5.00)............................... $ 10,000
    Cost in Assembly (2,000 × $1.174).............................   2,348   12,348
    Still in process:
    Cost in Machining (10,000 × $5.00)............................. $ 50,000
    Cost in Assembly:
      Materials..   –0–
      Labor (10,000 × 1/2 × $.616) $3,080
      Factory overhead (10,000 × 1/2 × $.308)...   1,540   4,620   54,620

Total production cost accounted for $301,580
*Total cost from preceding dept.:
    Work in process—beginning inventory .... $ 25,000
    Transferred in during period   225,000
      Total.. $250,000

    Total units from preceding dept.:
    Work in process—beginning inventory   5,000
    Transferred in during period   45,000
      Total..   50,000

  $250,000 ÷ 50,000 = $5 per unit

Part V

Chavez Chemical Company
Cost of Production Summary—Refining Department
For the Month of May 2002

Cost of work in process, beginning of month		$ 10,000
Cost of goods received from prior department during		
month		120,050
Cost of production for month:		
Materials	–0–	
Labor	$50,375	
Factory overhead	40,300	90,675
Total costs to be accounted for		$220,725***

	Labor and Factory Overhead
Unit output for month:	
To complete beginning units in process (10,000 × 50%)	5,000
Units started and finished during month..........................	30,000*
Ending units in process (7,000 × 75%)............................	5,250
Total equivalent production	40,250
Unit cost for month:	
Labor ($50,375 ÷ 40,250)...	$1.252
Factory overhead ($40,300 ÷ 40,250)..............................	1.001
Total	$2.253

Inventory costs:		
Cost of goods finished and transferred to Finishing		
Department during month:		
Beginning units in process:		
Prior month's cost	$10,000	
Current cost to complete:		
Labor (10,000 × 1/2 × $1.252)...........................	6,260	
Factory overhead (10,000 × 1/2 × $1.001)	5,005	$ 21,265
Units started and finished during month:		
Cost in prior department (30,000 × $3.245**)............	$97,350	
Cost in Refining Department (30,000 × $2.253).........	67,590	
Total cost transferred (30,000 × $5.77)		164,940
Cost of work in process, end of month:		
Cost in prior department (7,000 × $3.245)	$22,715	
Cost in Refining Department:		
Labor (7,000 × 3/4 × $1.252).......................................	6,573	
Factory overhead (7,000 × 3/4 × $1.001)	5,255	34,543
Total production costs accounted for................................		$220,748***
* Transferred to the finishing department.................................		40,000
Less units in beginning inventory...................................		10,000
Units started and completed during month...........................		30,000

** Cost transferred from prior department: $120,050 ÷ 37,000 = $3.245 adjusted unit cost

***Rounding difference

Part VI

1.

Product	Units	Unit Sales Price	Total Sales Value	Percent of Total	Assignment of Joint Costs
Sigma	15,000	$10	$150,000	75%	$75,000
Chi	10,000	$5	50,000	25%	25,000
Total	25,000		$200,000	100%	$100,000

2.

Product	Units	Unit Sales Price	Ultimate Sales Value	Cost After Split-off	Sales Value at Split-off	Percent of Total	Assignment of Joint Costs
Sigma	15,000	$10	$150,000	$45,000	$105,000	72.41%	$ 72,410
Chi	10,000	$5	50,000	10,000	40,000	27.59%	27,590
Total	25,000		$200,000	$55,000	$145,000	100.00%	$100,000

3.

Total costs to split-off point $100,000

Less market value of by-product................................. 10,000

Joint costs to be assigned to main products................ $ 90,000

Product

Sigma: $90,000 × 72.41%......................   = $ 65,169

Chi: 90,000 × 27.59% ....   =   24,831

Gamma ....   =   10,000

Total joint costs assigned $100,000

CHAPTER 7 SOLUTIONS

Part I

1. T	**6.** F	**11.** T
2. F	**7.** T	**12.** F
3. T	**8.** T	**13.** T
4. F	**9.** F	**14.** F
5. F	**10.** T	**15.** T

Part II

1. l	**5.** a	**9.** k
2. j	**6.** i	**10.** c
3. f	**7.** h	**11.** g
4. e	**8.** b	**12.** d
		13. m

Part III

1. (c) Attainable standards are set for a normal level of operation and efficiency, and are intended to represent challenging, yet attainable results. Theoretical standards are set for an ideal or maximum level of operation and efficiency. Practical capacity is theoretical capacity less allowance for unavoidable interruptions.

2. (b) If the aim is to isolate the materials price variance at the earliest possible time, it should be isolated at the time of purchase and called a purchase price variance.

3. (b) Standard rate × (Actual quantity – Standard quantity)
$1.30 × (6,400 – 6,000) = $520 unfav.

4. (c) $$\frac{\$40,000}{20,000 \text{ units}} = \$2$$

Actual quantity × (Actual price – Standard price)

20,000 × ($2.00 – $2.10) = $2,000 fav.

5. (b) Direct labor rate variance = Actual hours × (Actual rate – Standard rate)

34,500 × ($7.00* – $6.40) = $20,700 unfav.

*$241,500 × 34,500

6. (d) Direct labor efficiency variance = Standard rate × (Actual hours – Standard hours)
$10 × (2,000 – 1,800) = $2,000 unfav.

7. (a) The higher paid, more experienced workers had a higher wage rate, but they were more efficient.

8. (b) When actual hours exceed standard hours, a debit balance is created in the labor-efficiency variance account.

9. (b) If significant variances exist, inventory and cost of goods sold figures are not stated at actual cost in a standard cost system unless these variances are allocated prior to the preparation of the financial statements.

10. (d) The actual labor cost is more than the standard labor cost because the credit to Payroll, $11,000, is more than the debit to Work in Process, $10,000.

Part IV

1.

	Pounds	Unit Cost		Amount	
Actual quantity used	29,200	$1.10	Actual	$32,120	
Actual quantity used	29,200	1.00	Standard	29,200	
Materials price variance..........		$ .10		$ 2,920	unfavorable
Actual quantity used	29,200	$1.00	Standard	$29,200	
Standard quantity allowed					
(9,500 units × 3 lbs.)...........	28,500	1.00	Standard	28,500	
Materials quantity variance.....	700			$ 700	unfavorable

2.

	Time	Rate		Amount	
Actual hours worked..............	19,500	$14.50*	Actual	$282,750	
Actual hours worked..............	19,500	15.00	Standard	292,500	
Labor rate variance		$ .50		$ 9,750	favorable
Actual hours worked..............	19,500	$15.00	Standard	$292,500	
Standard hours allowed					
(9,500 units × 2 hrs.**).......	19,000	15.00	Standard	285,000	
Labor efficiency variance........	500			$ 7,500	unfavorable

   *$282,750 ÷ 19,500 = $14.50
   **20,000 hours ÷ 10,000 units = 2 hrs. per unit

3.

Actual quantity used × Actual price per unit	Actual quantity × Standard price per unit	Equivalent production × Standard quantity per unit × Standard price
29,200 lbs. × $1.10 = $32,120	29,200 × $1= $29,200	9,500 units × 3 lbs × $1 = $28,500
Materials Price Variance $2,920 unfav.		Materials Quantity Variance $700 unfav.

Net Materials Variance
$3,620 unfav.

Actual hours × Actual rate per hour	Actual hours × Standard rate per hour	Equivalent production × Standard hours per unit × Standard rate
19,500 hours × $14.50 = $282,750	19,500 hours × $15 = $292,500	9,500 units × 2 hours × $15 = $285,000
Labor Rate Variance $9,750 fav.		Labor Efficiency Variance $7,500 unfav.

Net Labor Variance
$2,250 fav.

Part V

1.	Materials	90,000	
	Materials Purchase Price Variance		900
	Accounts Payable		89,100
2.	Work in Process	74,250	
	Materials Quantity Variance	750	
	Materials		75,000
3.	Work in Process	78,400	
	Labor Efficiency Variance	1,000	
	Labor Rate Variance	600	
	Payroll		80,000
4.	Work in Process	60,000	
	Applied Factory Overhead		60,000
5.	Finished Goods	150,000	
	Work in Process		150,000

Part VI

Verdin Company
Income Statement
For Year Ended December 31, 2002

Sales..		$80,000
Cost of goods sold at standard	$50,000	
Add unfavorable variances:		
Materials price variance	820	
Labor rate variance	210	
	$51,030	
Less favorable variances:		
Labor efficiency variance	200	
Materials quantity variance	1,600	
Cost of goods sold (actual)...		49,230
Gross margin on sales (actual)......................................		$30,770

CHAPTER 8 SOLUTIONS

Part I

1. T	**6.** T	**11.** T
2. F	**7.** T	**12.** F
3. T	**8.** T	**13.** T
4. T	**9.** T	**14.** F
5. T	**10.** T	**15.** T

Part II

1. m	**8.** c	**15.** h
2. b	**9.** r	**16.** o
3. q	**10.** a	**17.** n
4. i	**11.** l	**18.** k
5. g	**12.** e	**19.** j
6. f	**13.** d	**20.** t
7. s	**14.** p	

Part III

1. (b) Overapplied overhead would result if factory overhead costs incurred were less than costs charged to production.

2. (c) Controllable variance = Actual overhead – Budgeted overhead at standard
Volume variance = Budgeted overhead at standard – Overhead applied

3. (c) The spending variance is a result of the prices paid for overhead items or the quantities used of overhead items being more or less than was budgeted for a given level of production.

4. (a) If factory overhead costs are mostly variable, changes in the level of production should have little effect on the amount of overhead cost applied to products.

5. (b) Net overhead variance = Actual overhead – Applied overhead

6. (b) The sales budget affects the planned expenditure level for selling and administrative expenses, whereas the production budget affects the planned expenditures for materials, labor, and factory overhead.

7. (c) Within a relevant range, fixed costs remain the same in total, and they increase per unit as volume decreases and decrease per unit as volume increases.

8. (d)

Total overhead application rate per direct labor hour...................	$3.00
Budgeted fixed costs of $9,000 ÷ 18,000 normal direct labor hours = fixed cost application rate per hour	.50
Variable overhead application rate per hour	$2.50
Standard hours allowed	×15,000
Variable overhead costs budgeted	$37,500
Budgeted fixed costs...	9,000
	$46,500

Overhead applied (15,000 hours × $3.00) $45,000

$1,500
Volume
variance
(Unfavorable)

9. (b) Budgeted overhead—fixed .... $ 9,000
Budgeted overhead—variable 37,500 $46,500

$6,250
Controllable
variance
(Favorable)

Actual total overhead $40,250

10. (b) Fixed costs budgeted .... $ 3,500.00
Actual hours 1,750
Variable overhead rate per hour .... ×$1.25
Variable overhead budgeted 2,187.50
Total overhead budgeted .... $ 5,687.50
Actual overhead 7,500.00
Unfavorable spending variance .... $(1,812.50)

Part IV

Factory Expense Category	Budget Rate	Level of Activity (Direct Labor Hours)			
		45,000	50,000	55,000	60,000
Variable costs (per direct labor hour):					
Indirect labor	$2.00	$90,000	$100,000	$110,000	$120,000
Indirect materials	.80	36,000	40,000	44,000	48,000
Repairs	.60	27,000	30,000	33,000	36,000
Total variable cost	$3.40	$153,000	$170,000	$187,000	$204,000
Fixed costs (total):					
Depreciation—machinery	$50,000	$ 50,000	$ 50,000	$ 50,000	$ 50,000
Insurance—factory	25,000	25,000	25,000	25,000	25,000
Total fixed cost	$75,000	$ 75,000	$ 75,000	$ 75,000	$ 75,000
Total overhead budget		$228,000	$245,000	$262,000	$279,000
Factory overhead rate per direct labor hour		$5.067	$4.900	$4.764	$4.650
Fixed overhead rate per direct labor hour		$1.667	$1.500	$1.364	$1.250

Part V

1. Actual factory overhead... $163,000
   Applied factory overhead $7.50/DLH × (20,000 × 110%) 165,000
   Over- or underapplied factory overhead................................. $ 2,000 overerapplied

2. Actual factory overhead... $163,000
   Overhead for capacity attained:
      Fixed factory overhead .... $ 50,000
      Variable factory overhead (110% × $100,000) 110,000   160,000
   Controllable variance .... $ 3,000 unfav.
   Factory overhead for capacity attained........................... $160,000
   Factory overhead applied   165,000
   Volume variance... $ 5,000 fav.

Part VI

1. Actual factory overhead... $117,000
   Budget allowance based on standard hours allowed:
      Fixed overhead budgeted... $20,000
      Variable overhead (9,500 × 2 hrs.* × $5).................... 95,000   115,000
         Controllable variance .... $ 2,000 unfav.
   Budget allowance based on standard hours allowed....... $115,000
   Overhead charged to production (9,500 × 2 hrs.) ×
      ($1** fixed + $5 variable)   114,000
      Volume variance .... $ 1,000 unfav.

     *20,000 hours ÷ 10,000 units = 2 hours per unit
   **$20,000 ÷ 20,000 hours = $1 per hour

2. Actual variable factory overhead................................... $97,000
   Budget allowance based on actual hours worked:
      Variable overhead (19,500 × $5)...............................   97,500
         Spending variance .... $ 500 fav.
   Actual hours × standard variable overhead rate $97,500
   Variable overhead charged to production (19,500 × $5).   95,000
      Efficiency variance .... $ 2,500 unfav.
   Actual fixed cost ($117,000 − $97,000) $20,000
   Budgeted fixed cost..   20,000
      Budget variance ....   –0–
   Budgeted fixed cost.. $20,000
   Standard hours × fixed rate (19,000 × $1).....................   19,000
      Volume variance .... $ 1,000 unfav.

Part VII

1.

	Socks	Shorts	Handkerchiefs
Units required to meet sales budget.........	50,000	25,000	75,000
Add desired ending inventories	2,500	2,000	5,000
Total units required...............................	52,500	27,000	80,000
Less estimated beginning inventories........	3,000	1,000	4,000
Planned production	49,500	26,000	76,000

2.

	Rayon	Cotton
Socks...	198,000	99,000
Shorts..	130,000	–0–
Handkerchiefs...	–0–	228,000
Total...	328,000	327,000
Add desired ending inventories	7,500	6,000
Total...	335,500	333,000
Less estimated beginning inventories...................	6,000	5,000
Budgeted quantities of materials purchases	329,500	328,000
Budgeted purchase price per pound.........................	× $.75	× $.50
Budgeted dollar amounts of materials purchases..............	$247,125	$164,000

CHAPTER 9 SOLUTIONS

Part I

1. F	6. T	11. F
2. T	7. T	12. T
3. F	8. F	13. T
4. T	9. F	14. T
5. T	10. T	15. T

Part II

1. g	5. i	8. c
2. a	6. b	9. f
3. j	7. h	10. e
4. d		

Part III

1. (b) Approximately 70% of U.S. workers are employed in the service sector.

2. (a) Answers (b) through (d) are examples of service businesses, whereas (a) is a manufacturer of beverages.

3. (d) Approximately 90% of jobs created in the U.S. in the last 20 years have been in service industries.

4. (c) The basic document used to accumulate costs for a service business using job order costing is the job order cost sheet.

5. (a) If the more highly paid partners control most of the secretarial support services, professional labor dollars would be the most appropriate allocation base.

6. (a) The budgeted income statement is the end point for the annual budget because all of the other budgets must be completed before it can be prepared.

7. (d) Meals and travel would be examples of direct expenses that could readily be traced to individual jobs by keeping a log of travel expenses by job.

8. (c) A cost performance report compares the budgeted costs for a job to the actual costs and indicates a variance for each line item.

9. (a) Firms that use activity-based costing attempt to shift as many costs as possible out of indirect cost pools and specifically trace them to individual jobs.

10. (b) Peanut-butter costing refers to the practice of assigning costs evenly to jobs using an overhead rate, even though different jobs consume resources in different proportions.

Part IV

1.

Billick and Fischer
Revenue Budget
For the Year Ended December 31, 2002

Item	Professional Hours	Billing Rate	Total Revenues
Partners	2,000	$200	$ 400,000
Associates	7,000	120	840,000
Staff	11,000	80	880,000
Total	20,000		$2,120,000

2.

Billick and Fischer
Professional Labor Budget
For the Year Ended December 31, 2002

Item	Professional Hours	Wage Rate	Total Labor Dollars
Partners	2,000	$100	$ 200,000
Associates	7,000	60	420,000
Staff	11,000	40	440,000
Total	20,000		$1,060,000

3.

Billick and Fischer
Overhead Budget
For the Year Ended December 31, 2002

Item	Amount
Secretarial Support	$230,000
Fringe Benefits	190,000
Depreciation—Building	90,000
Utilities	43,000
Depreciation—Equipment	40,000
Telephone/Fax	31,000
Photocopying	22,000
Total	$646,000

4.

Billick and Fischer
Other Expenses Budget
For the Year Ended December 31, 2002

Item	Amount
Travel	$54,000
Meals	18,000
Total	$72,000

5.

Billick and Fischer
Budgeted Income Statement
For the Year Ended December 31, 2002

Revenues		$2,120,000
Operating Costs:		
Professional Labor	$1,060,000	
Overhead Support	646,000	
Other Expenses	72,000	1,778,000
Operating Income		$ 342,000

Part V

1.

	Ajax Industries	Richard Stevens
Professional Labor Cost:		
50 hrs. × $57.14*..................................	$2,857	
45 hrs. × $57.14...................................		$2,571
Professional Support:		
50 hrs. × $39.05**................................	1,953	
45 hrs. × $39.05...................................		1,757
Total..	$4,810	$4,328

Computations:

$$* \frac{(\$125,000 \times 2) + (\$70,000 \times 5)}{1,500 \times 7} = \$57.14$$

$$** \frac{\$410,000}{10,500 \text{ hrs.}} = \$39.05$$

2.

	Ajax Industries	Richard Stevens
Professional Labor Cost:		
10 hrs. × $83.33*..................................	$ 833	
30 hrs. × $83.33...................................		$2,500
Associate Labor Cost:		
40 hrs. × $46.67**................................	1,867	
15 hrs. × $46.67...................................		700
Litigation Support:		
$833 × $1.12***	933	
$2,500 × $1.12		2,800
Secretarial Support:		
50 hrs. × $12.38****	619	
45 hrs. × $12.38...................................		557
Total..	$4,252	$6,557

Computations:

$$* \frac{(2 \times \$125,000)}{1,500 \times 2} = \$83.33$$

$$** \frac{5 \times \$70,000}{1,500 \times 5} = \$46.67$$

$$*** \frac{\$280,000}{(2 \times \$125,000)} = \$1.12$$

$$**** \frac{\$130,000}{(7 \times 1,500)} = \$12.38$$

CHAPTER 10
SOLUTIONS

Part I

1. F	6. T	11. T
2. T	7. T	12. F
3. F	8. F	13. T
4. T	9. T	14. F
5. T	10. T	15. F

Part II

1. d	6. h	11. o
2. i	7. l	12. g
3. a	8. b	13. m
4. k	9. e	14. n
5. c	10. j	15. f

Part III

1. (a) Under direct costing, it is necessary to know the variable and fixed components of all production costs because variable manufacturing costs are treated as product costs, whereas fixed manufacturing costs are treated as period costs for income determination purposes.

2. (d) In absorption costing, fixed manufacturing expenses form part of the predetermined factory overhead rate and are included in inventories. The exclusion of this overhead from inventories under direct costing and its offsetting effect on periodic income determination has been criticized by opponents of direct costing.

3. (b) A decrease in ending inventory causes fewer costs to be inventoried under absorption costing than under direct costing due to the fixed manufacturing element. The smaller the ending inventory, the larger the cost of goods sold and the smaller the operating income under absorption costing.

4. (a)
Operating income (direct costing)	$50,000
Cost released in inventory decrease (5,000 units × $1)	5,000
Operating income (absorption costing)	$45,000

5. (c) $\dfrac{\$200,000 + \$40,000}{\$8 - \$4} = \dfrac{\$240,000}{\$4} = 60,000$ units

6. (a) The contribution margin as a percentage of sales will decrease because the variable cost as a percentage of sales increases. If the fixed cost increases and the contribution margin ratio decreases, both of these factors will cause the break-even point to increase.

7. (b) The contribution margin ratio is needed to compute target volume sales dollars, which is obtained by dividing the sales price per unit into the contribution margin per unit (Sales price per unit – Variable cost per unit).

8. (b)

	Regular Sales	Special Order	Total
Sales	$1,500,000	$1,350,000	$2,850,000
Variable costs.........................	825,000	825,000	1,650,000
Contribution margin	$ 675,000	$ 525,000	$1,200,000
Fixed costs			495,000
Operating income			$ 705,000

9. (a)

Direct materials	$ 4
Direct labor	5
Variable overhead (1/3 × $6)..	2
Shipping costs..	3
Minimum selling price	$14

10. (c)   The sales price should exceed the variable cost of making and selling the product.

Part IV

Flashpoint Manufacturing Company
Income Statement
For the Month Ended July 31, 2002

	Absorption Costing	Direct Costing
Sales	$160,000	$160,000
Cost of goods sold...	(120,000)	(96,000)
Underapplied/overapplied factory overhead*	11,000	
Gross margin	$ 51,000	
Contribution margin..		$ 64,000
Less:		
Fixed factory overhead...		(25,000)**
Selling and administrative expenses	(25,000)	(25,000)
Net income (loss)	$ 26,000	$ 14,000

*Calculation of overapplied fixed factory overhead:	
Fixed factory overhead per year (50,000 × $6)	$300,000
**Fixed factory overhead per month ($300,000 ÷ 12)..............................	$ 25,000
Fixed factory overhead applied to production (6,000 × $6)...................	$ 36,000
Fixed overhead per month..	25,000
Fixed factory overhead overapplied...	$ 11,000

Flashpoint Manufacturing Company
Income Statement
For the Month Ended August 31, 2002

	Absorption Costing	Direct Costing
Sales	$240,000	$240,000
Cost of goods sold	(180,000)	(144,000)
Underapplied/overapplied factory overhead*	(1,000)	
Gross margin	$ 59,000	
Contribution margin		$ 96,000
Less:		
Fixed factory overhead		(25,000)
Selling and administrative expenses	(25,000)	(25,000)
Net income (loss)	$ 34,000	$ 46,000

*Calculation of underapplied factory overhead:

Fixed factory overhead applied to production (4,000 × $6)	$24,000
Fixed factory overhead per month	25,000
Fixed factory overhead underapplied	$ (1,000)

Part V

1. $$\frac{\$80,000}{1 - \dfrac{\$60}{\$150}} = \frac{\$80,000}{.60} = \$133,333$$

2. $$\frac{\$80,000}{\$150 - \$60} = 889 \text{ units}$$

3. Margin of safety = 1,600 − 889 = 711 units

    $$\text{Margin of safety ratio} = \frac{1,600 - 889}{1,600} = 44\%$$

5. $$\text{Target volume} = \frac{\$80,000 + \$10,000/1 - .3}{\$150 - \$60}$$

    $$= 1,048 \text{ units}$$

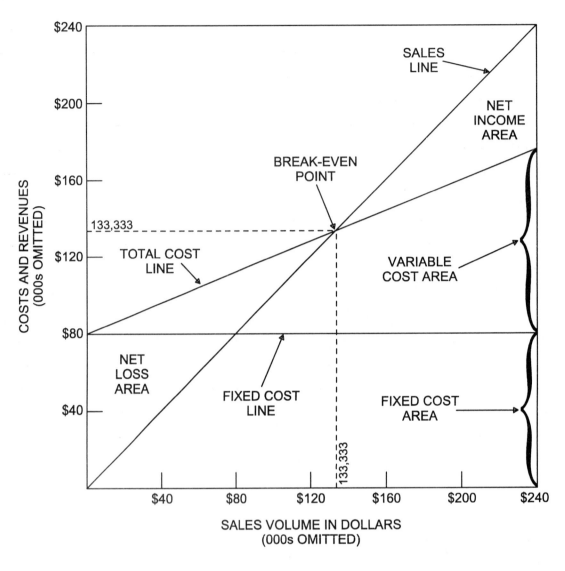

Part VI

1. The company should not accept the special order because the proposed $8.00 sales price does not cover all variable manufacturing costs per unit, which are:

Direct materials	$4.00
Direct labor	2.50
Variable factory overhead..............................	2.00
Total...	$8.50

Note: The assumption is that the variable marketing expense of $.50 per unit will not be incurred for this order because the buyer initiated the sale.

2. The company would be willing to pay an outside supplier as much as the variable manufacturing cost of $8.50 per unit plus the $.25 per unit ($2,500 ÷ 10,000) of fixed cost that would be saved, or $8.75 per unit.

(1) and (2)

(1)   Fiorelli Furniture Company

Statement of Cost of Goods Manufactured

For the Month Ended September 30, 2002

(2)

Fiorelli Furniture Company
Income Statement
For the Month Ended September 30, 2002

(3)

Fiorelli Furniture Company

Balance Sheet

September 30, 2002

(1)

JOURNAL

	DESCRIPTION	DEBIT	CREDIT	
1				1
2				2
3				3
4				4
5				5
6				6
7				7
8				8
9				9
10				10
11				11
12				12
13				13
14				14
15				15
16				16
17				17
18				18
19				19
20				20
21				21
22				22
23				23
24				24
25				25
26				26
27				27
28				28
29				29
30				30
31				31
32				32
33				33
34				34
35				35
36				36

JOURNAL

	DESCRIPTION	DEBIT	CREDIT	
1				1
2				2
3				3
4				4
5				5
6				6
7				7
8				8
9				9
10				10
11				11
12				12
13				13
14				14
15				15
16				16
17				17
18				18
19				19
20				20
21				21
22				22
23				23
24				24
25				25
26				26
27				27
28				28
29				29
30				30
31				31
32				32
33				33
34				34
35				35
36				36

(2)

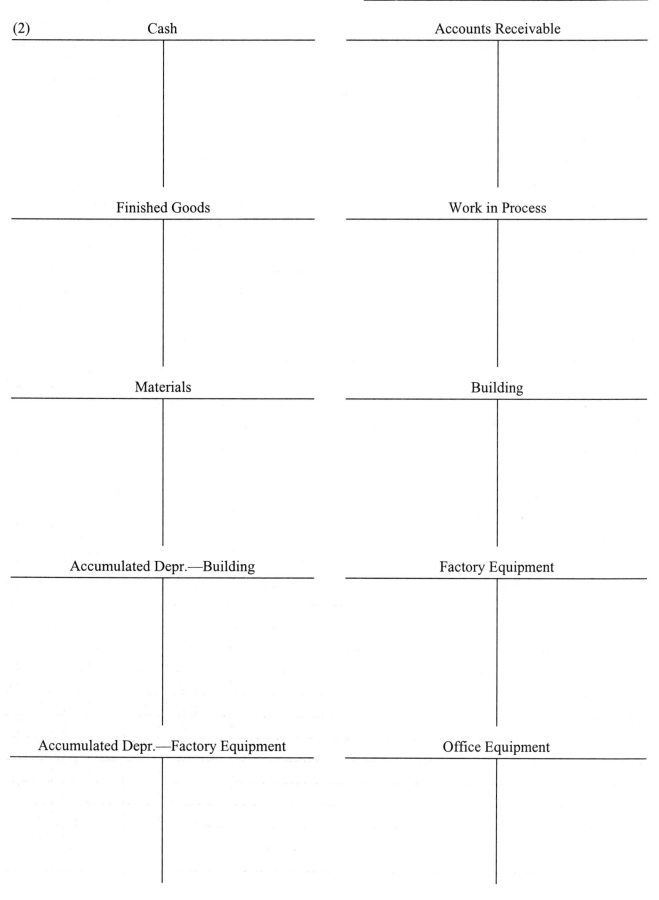

Cash	Accounts Receivable
Finished Goods	Work in Process
Materials	Building
Accumulated Depr.—Building	Factory Equipment
Accumulated Depr.—Factory Equipment	Office Equipment

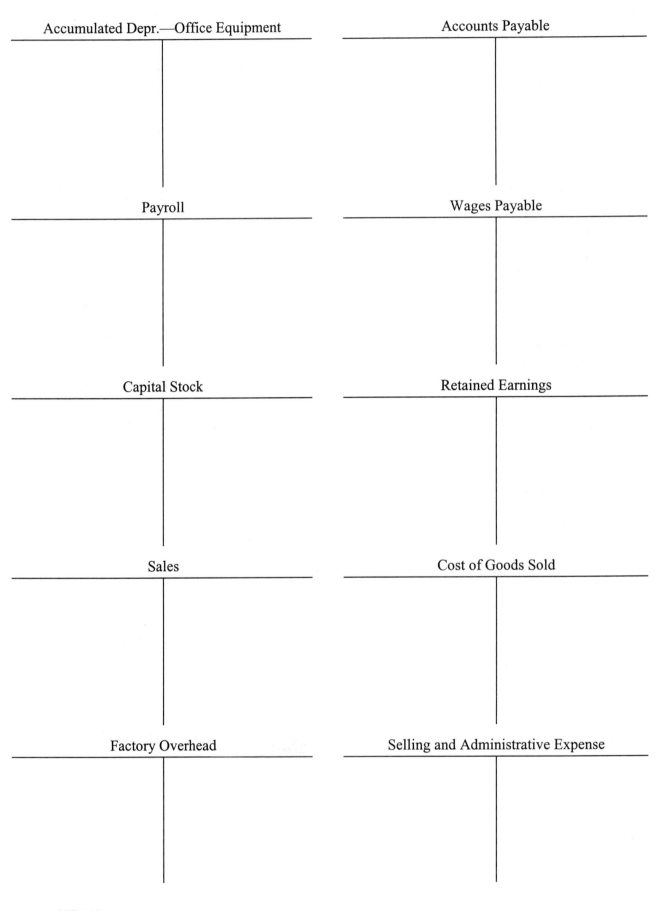

Accumulated Depr.—Office Equipment

Accounts Payable

Payroll

Wages Payable

Capital Stock

Retained Earnings

Sales

Cost of Goods Sold

Factory Overhead

Selling and Administrative Expense

(3)   Mountain Manufacturing Co.

Statement of Cost of Goods Manufactured

For the Month Ended May 31, 2002

Mountain Manufacturing Co.

Income Statement

For the Month Ended May 31, 2002

Mountain Manufacturing Co.

Balance Sheet

May 31, 2002

Name _____

(1)–(10)

JOURNAL

PAGE

	DESCRIPTION	DEBIT	CREDIT	
1				1
2				2
3				3
4				4
5				5
6				6
7				7
8				8
9				9
10				10
11				11
12				12
13				13
14				14
15				15
16				16
17				17
18				18
19				19
20				20
21				21
22				22
23				23
24				24
25				25
26				26
27				27
28				28
29				29
30				30
31				31
32				32
33				33
34				34
35				35
36				36

PROBLEM 1-4, Concluded

JOURNAL

	DESCRIPTION	DEBIT	CREDIT	
1				1
2				2
3				3
4				4
5				5
6				6
7				7
8				8
9				9
10				10
11				11
12				12
13				13
14				14
15				15
16				16
17				17
18				18
19				19
20				20
21				21
22				22
23				23
24				24
25				25
26				26
27				27
28				28
29				29
30				30
31				31
32				32
33				33
34				34
35				35
36				36

(1), (3), and (4)

PROBLEM 1–5, Concluded

(2)

JOURNAL

	DESCRIPTION	DEBIT	CREDIT	
1				1
2				2
3				3
4				4
5				5
6				6
7				7
8				8
9				9
10				10
11				11
12				12
13				13
14				14
15				15
16				16
17				17
18				18
19				19
20				20
21				21
22				22
23				23
24				24
25				25
26				26
27				27
28				28
29				29
30				30
31				31
32				32
33				33
34				34
35				35
36				36

(1)

Marino Manufacturing Company

Statement of Cost of Goods Manufactured

For the Month Ended July 31, 20--

(2)   Marino Manufacturing Company

Schedule to Compute Prime Cost

For the Month Ended July 31, 20--

(3)   Marino Manufacturing Company

Schedule to Compute Conversion Cost

For the Month Ended July 31, 20--

(1)

JOURNAL

	DESCRIPTION	DEBIT	CREDIT	
1				1
2				2
3				3
4				4
5				5
6				6
7				7
8				8
9				9
10				10
11				11
12				12
13				13
14				14
15				15
16				16
17				17
18				18
19				19
20				20
21				21
22				22
23				23
24				24
25				25
26				26
27				27
28				28
29				29
30				30
31				31
32				32
33				33
34				34
35				35
36				36

(2)(a)

(2)(b)

(2)(c)

(1) and (3)

JOURNAL

	DESCRIPTION	DEBIT	CREDIT	
1				1
2				2
3				3
4				4
5				5
6				6
7				7
8				8
9				9
10				10
11				11
12				12
13				13
14				14
15				15
16				16
17				17
18				18
19				19
20				20
21				21
22				22
23				23
24				24
25				25
26				26
27				27
28				28
29				29
30				30
31				31
32				32
33				33
34				34
35				35
36				36

(2)

(4)

The High-P Manufacturing Company

Statement of Cost of Goods Manufactured

For the Month Ended September 30, 20--

Name _____

Little Rock Corporation
Statement of Cost of Goods Manufactured
For the Month Ended September 30, 20--

PROBLEM 1-9, Concluded

Supporting Computations:

(1), (2), and (3) _____

Name _____

STORES LEDGER

(1)(a) FIFO costing

Description _____

Stores Ledger Account No. _____

Date	RECEIVED				ISSUED					BALANCE		
	Rec. Rep. No.	Quantity	Unit Price	Amount	Mat. Req. No.	Quantity	Unit Price	Amount	Quantity	Unit Price	Amount

(1)(b) LIFO costing

STORES LEDGER

Description _____

Stores Ledger Account No. _____

Date	RECEIVED				ISSUED					BALANCE		
	Rec. Rep. No.	Quantity	Unit Price	Amount	Mat. Req. No.	Quantity	Unit Price	Amount		Quantity	Unit Price	Amount

Name _____

(1)(c) Moving average costing

STORES LEDGER

Description _____

Stores Ledger
Account No. _____

Date	RECEIVED					ISSUED					BALANCE		
	Rec. Rep. No.	Quantity	Unit Price	Amount		Mat. Req. No.	Quantity	Unit Price	Amount		Quantity	Unit Price	Amount

PROBLEM 2–2, Concluded

(2), (3), and (4)

(1) FIFO method

STORES LEDGER

Description _____

Stores Ledger
Account No. _____

Date	RECEIVED				ISSUED				BALANCE		
	Rec. Rep. No.	Quantity	Unit Price	Amount	Mat. Req. No.	Quantity	Unit Price	Amount	Quantity	Unit Price	Amount

(2) LIFO method

Description _____

STORES LEDGER

Stores Ledger
Account No. _____

Date	RECEIVED				ISSUED				BALANCE		
	Rec. Rep. No.	Quantity	Unit Price	Amount	Mat. Req. No.	Quantity	Unit Price	Amount	Quantity	Unit Price	Amount

(3) Moving average method

STORES LEDGER

Description _____

Stores Ledger Account No. _____

Date	Rec. Rep. No.	RECEIVED Quantity	RECEIVED Unit Price	RECEIVED Amount	Mat. Req. No.	ISSUED Quantity	ISSUED Unit Price	ISSUED Amount	BALANCE Quantity	BALANCE Unit Price	BALANCE Amount

(1)

JOURNAL   PAGE

	DESCRIPTION	DEBIT	CREDIT	
1				1
2				2
3				3
4				4
5				5
6				6
7				7
8				8
9				9
10				10
11				11
12				12
13				13
14				14
15				15
16				16
17				17
18				18
19				19
20				20
21				21
22				22
23				23
24				24
25				25
26				26
27				27
28				28
29				29
30				30
31				31
32				32
33				33
34				34
35				35
36				36

PROBLEM 2–4, Concluded

(2)

Cash

Accounts Payable

Materials

Factory Overhead

Work in Process

(3)

(1) and (2)

(3)

(1)

Date	(a) Form Used	(b) Journal Entry	(c) Book of Original Entry Used	(d) Subsidiary Records Affected

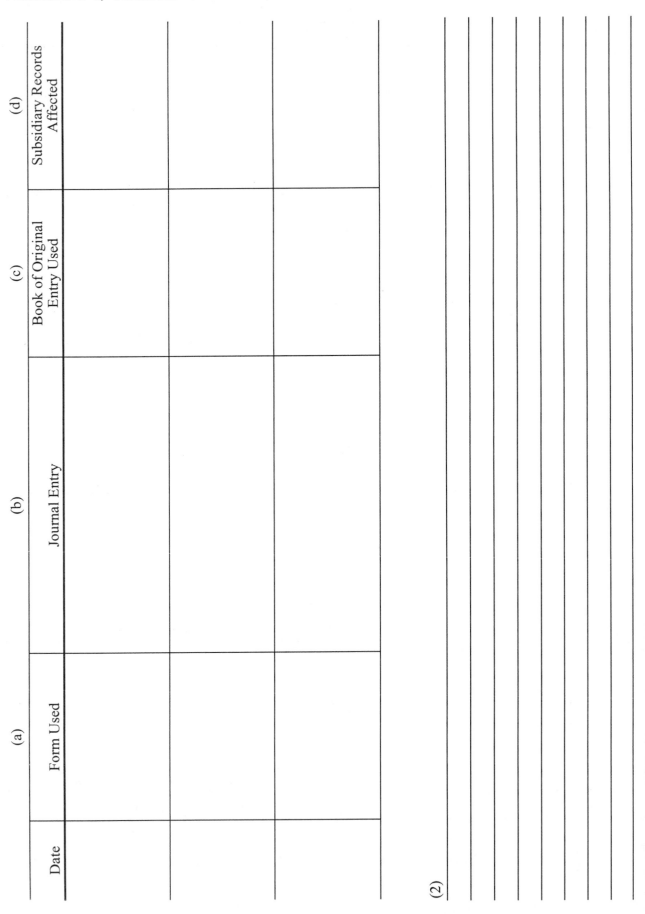

Date	(a) Form Used	(b) Journal Entry	(c) Book of Original Entry Used	(d) Subsidiary Records Affected

(2)

(1) and (3)   Cash   Factory Supplies

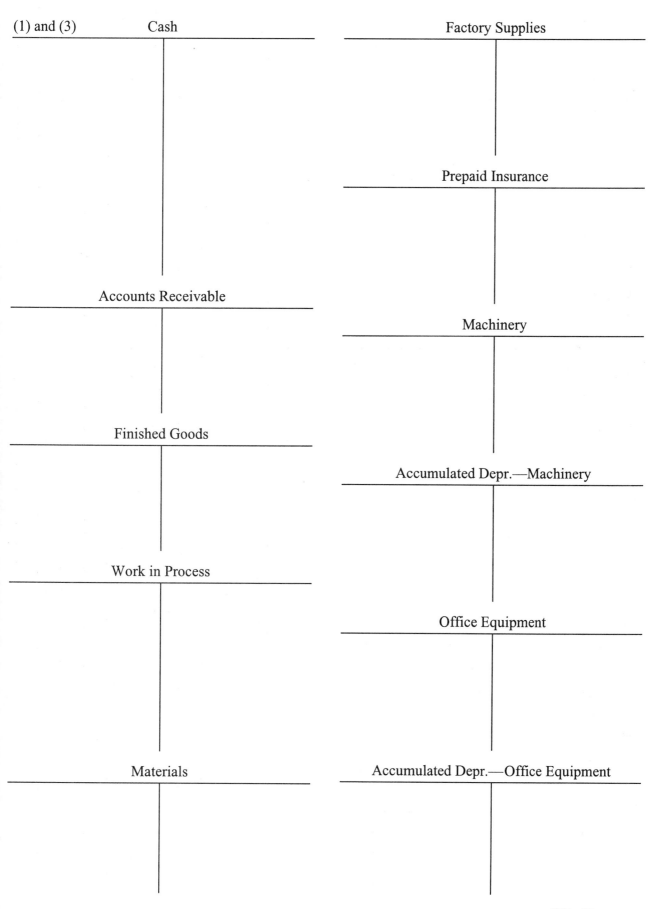

              Accounts Receivable   Machinery

               Finished Goods   Accumulated Depr.—Machinery

               Work in Process   Office Equipment

                 Materials   Accumulated Depr.—Office Equipment

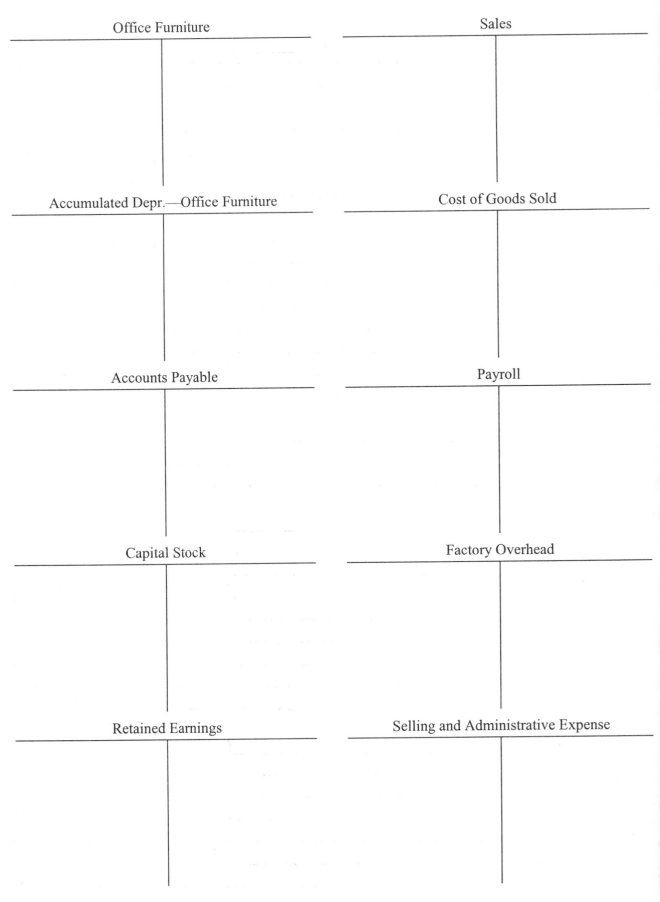

Office Furniture

Sales

Accumulated Depr.—Office Furniture

Cost of Goods Sold

Accounts Payable

Payroll

Capital Stock

Factory Overhead

Retained Earnings

Selling and Administrative Expense

(2)

JOURNAL

	DESCRIPTION	DEBIT	CREDIT	
1				1
2				2
3				3
4				4
5				5
6				6
7				7
8				8
9				9
10				10
11				11
12				12
13				13
14				14
15				15
16				16
17				17
18				18
19				19
20				20
21				21
22				22
23				23
24				24
25				25
26				26
27				27
28				28
29				29
30				30
31				31
32				32
33				33
34				34
35				35
36				36

JOURNAL

PAGE

	DESCRIPTION	DEBIT	CREDIT	
1				1
2				2
3				3
4				4
5				5
6				6
7				7
8				8
9				9
10				10
11				11
12				12
13				13
14				14
15				15
16				16
17				17
18				18
19				19
20				20
21				21
22				22
23				23
24				24
25				25
26				26
27				27
28				28
29				29
30				30
31				31
32				32
33				33
34				34
35				35
36				36

(4)   Lift-Up Inc.

Statement of Cost of Goods Manufactured

For the Month Ended October 31, 20--

(5)

Lift-Up Inc.

Income Statement

For the Month Ended October 31, 20--

(6)   Lift-Up Inc.

Balance Sheet

October 31, 20--

Name _____

JOURNAL

PAGE _____

	DESCRIPTION	DEBIT	CREDIT	
1				1
2				2
3				3
4				4
5				5
6				6
7				7
8				8
9				9
10				10
11				11
12				12
13				13
14				14
15				15
16				16
17				17
18				18
19				19
20				20
21				21
22				22
23				23
24				24
25				25
26				26
27				27
28				28
29				29
30				30
31				31
32				32
33				33
34				34
35				35
36				36

JOURNAL

PAGE

	DESCRIPTION	DEBIT	CREDIT	
1				1
2				2
3				3
4				4
5				5
6				6
7				7
8				8
9				9
10				10
11				11
12				12
13				13
14				14
15				15
16				16
17				17
18				18
19				19
20				20
21				21
22				22
23				23
24				24
25				25
26				26
27				27
28				28
29				29
30				30
31				31
32				32
33				33
34				34
35				35
36				36

(1) and (2)

JOURNAL

	DESCRIPTION	DEBIT	CREDIT	
1				1
2				2
3				3
4				4
5				5
6				6
7				7
8				8
9				9
10				10
11				11
12				12
13				13
14				14
15				15
16				16
17				17
18				18
19				19
20				20
21				21
22				22
23				23
24				24
25				25
26				26
27				27
28				28
29				29
30				30
31				31
32				32
33				33
34				34
35				35
36				36

JOURNAL

	DESCRIPTION	DEBIT	CREDIT	
1				1
2				2
3				3
4				4
5				5
6				6
7				7
8				8
9				9
10				10
11				11
12				12
13				13
14				14
15				15
16				16
17				17
18				18
19				19
20				20
21				21
22				22
23				23
24				24
25				25
26				26
27				27
28				28
29				29
30				30
31				31
32				32
33				33
34				34
35				35
36				36

Name _____

(1)–(4)

JOURNAL

PAGE _____

	DESCRIPTION	DEBIT	CREDIT	
1				1
2				2
3				3
4				4
5				5
6				6
7				7
8				8
9				9
10				10
11				11
12				12
13				13
14				14
15				15
16				16
17				17
18				18
19				19
20				20
21				21
22				22
23				23
24				24
25				25
26				26
27				27
28				28
29				29
30				30
31				31
32				32
33				33
34				34
35				35
36				36

PROBLEM 2-10, Concluded

JOURNAL

	DESCRIPTION	DEBIT	CREDIT	
1				1
2				2
3				3
4				4
5				5
6				6
7				7
8				8
9				9
10				10
11				11
12				12
13				13
14				14
15				15
16				16
17				17
18				18
19				19
20				20
21				21
22				22
23				23
24				24
25				25
26				26
27				27
28				28
29				29
30				30
31				31
32				32
33				33
34				34
35				35
36				36

(1)–(5)

Name _____

JOURNAL

	DESCRIPTION	DEBIT	CREDIT	
1				1
2				2
3				3
4				4
5				5
6				6
7				7
8				8
9				9
10				10
11				11
12				12
13				13
14				14
15				15
16				16
17				17
18				18
19				19
20				20
21				21
22				22
23				23
24				24
25				25
26				26
27				27
28				28
29				29
30				30
31				31
32				32
33				33
34				34
35				35
36				36

JOURNAL

PAGE

	DESCRIPTION	DEBIT	CREDIT	
1				1
2				2
3				3
4				4
5				5
6				6
7				7
8				8
9				9
10				10
11				11
12				12
13				13
14				14
15				15
16				16
17				17
18				18
19				19
20				20
21				21
22				22
23				23
24				24
25				25
26				26
27				27
28				28
29				29
30				30
31				31
32				32
33				33
34				34
35				35
36				36

(1), (2), and (3) _____

Name _____

(1)

Employees	Hours	Regular Earnings	Overtime Premium	Idle Time (Included in Reg. Earnings)	Total Earnings	FICA 8%	Income Tax 18%	Net Earnings

(2) and (3)

JOURNAL

	DESCRIPTION	DEBIT	CREDIT	
1				1
2				2
3				3
4				4
5				5
6				6
7				7
8				8
9				9
10				10
11				11
12				12
13				13
14				14
15				15
16				16
17				17
18				18
19				19
20				20
21				21
22				22
23				23
24				24
25				25
26				26
27				27
28				28
29				29
30				30
31				31
32				32
33				33
34				34
35				35
36				36

(4)

Distribution of labor cost to vans using calculated average labor rate:

(1)

Classification of Wages and Salaries	Total Earnings for Month	FICA Tax 8%	Unemployment Taxes		Total Payroll Taxes Imposed on Employer
			Federal Tax 1%	State Tax 4%	
Direct labor	88,180.00				
Indirect labor	16,220.00				
Total taxes on factory wages					
Administrative salaries	12,000.00				
Sales salaries	11,500.00				
Total payroll taxes					

Computations:

_____

_____

_____

_____

_____

_____

_____

_____

_____

_____

_____

_____

_____

_____

_____

_____

_____

_____

_____

_____

(2)

JOURNAL

	DESCRIPTION	DEBIT	CREDIT	
1				1
2				2
3				3
4				4
5				5
6				6
7				7
8				8
9				9
10				10
11				11
12				12
13				13
14				14
15				15
16				16
17				17
18				18
19				19
20				20
21				21
22				22
23				23
24				24
25				25
26				26
27				27
28				28
29				29
30				30
31				31
32				32
33				33
34				34
35				35
36				36

(1) _____

(2)

JOURNAL

PAGE

	DESCRIPTION	DEBIT	CREDIT	
1				1
2				2
3				3
4				4
5				5
6				6
7				7
8				8
9				9
10				10
11				11
12				12
13				13
14				14
15				15
16				16
17				17
18				18
19				19
20				20
21				21
22				22
23				23
24				24
25				25
26				26
27				27
28				28
29				29
30				30
31				31
32				32
33				33
34				34
35				35
36				36

(1) and (2)

JOURNAL

	DESCRIPTION	DEBIT	CREDIT	
1				1
2				2
3				3
4				4
5				5
6				6
7				7
8				8
9				9
10				10
11				11
12				12
13				13
14				14
15				15
16				16
17				17
18				18
19				19
20				20
21				21
22				22
23				23
24				24
25				25
26				26
27				27
28				28
29				29
30				30
31				31
32				32
33				33
34				34
35				35
36				36

(3)

(1)

Employee	Earnings Per Week			Total Earnings Through Fortieth Week	FICA Taxable Earnings	FICA	Income Tax Withheld	Net Earnings
	Regular	Overtime Premium	Total					

PROBLEM 3-6, Concluded

(2) and (3)

JOURNAL

	DESCRIPTION	DEBIT	CREDIT	
1				1
2				2
3				3
4				4
5				5
6				6
7				7
8				8
9				9
10				10
11				11
12				12
13				13
14				14
15				15
16				16
17				17
18				18
19				19
20				20
21				21
22				22
23				23
24				24
25				25
26				26
27				27
28				28
29				29
30				30
31				31
32				32
33				33
34				34
35				35
36				36

(1)–(5)

EMPLOYEE EARNINGS RECORDS

(1)

Employee's Name	Week Ending	Weekly Gross Earnings	Accumulated Gross Earnings	Weekly Earnings Subject to FICA	Withholdings		Net Amount Paid
					FICA Tax	Income Tax	

PROBLEM 3–8, Continued

(2)

PAYROLL RECORD

| Employee's Name | Gross Earnings | Withholdings | | Net Amount Paid |
		FICA Tax	Income Tax	

(3)   Labor Cost Summary
For the Month Ended November 30, 20--

Week Ending	Dr. Work in Process (Direct Labor)	Dr. Factory Overhead (Indirect Labor)	Dr. Admin. Salaries (Office)	Cr. Payroll (Total)

(4)

JOURNAL   PAGE

	DESCRIPTION	DEBIT	CREDIT	
1				1
2				2
3				3
4				4
5				5
6				6
7				7
8				8
9				9
10				10
11				11
12				12
13				13
14				14
15				15
16				16
17				17
18				18
19				19
20				20
21				21
22				22
23				23

PROBLEM 3–8, Concluded

PAGE

	DESCRIPTION	DEBIT	CREDIT	
1				1
2				2
3				3
4				4
5				5
6				6
7				7
8				8
9				9
10				10
11				11
12				12
13				13
14				14
15				15
16				16
17				17
18				18
19				19
20				20
21				21
22				22
23				23
24				24
25				25
26				26
27				27
28				28
29				29
30				30
31				31
32				32
33				33
34				34
35				35
36				36

(1)

Items	Taxable Earnings	FICA Tax 8%	Federal Unemploy- ment Tax 1%	State Unemploy- ment Tax 4%	Total Payroll Taxes
Factory wages					
Administrative salaries					
Sales salaries					

Computations:

_____

_____

_____

_____

_____

_____

_____

_____

_____

_____

_____

_____

_____

_____

_____

_____

_____

_____

_____

_____

_____

_____

_____

_____

_____

_____

(2)

JOURNAL

	DESCRIPTION	DEBIT	CREDIT	
1				1
2				2
3				3
4				4
5				5
6				6
7				7
8				8
9				9
10				10
11				11
12				12
13				13
14				14
15				15
16				16
17				17
18				18
19				19
20				20
21				21
22				22
23				23
24				24
25				25
26				26
27				27
28				28
29				29
30				30
31				31
32				32
33				33
34				34
35				35
36				36

Name _____

JOURNAL

PAGE

	DESCRIPTION	DEBIT	CREDIT	
1				1
2				2
3				3
4				4
5				5
6				6
7				7
8				8
9				9
10				10
11				11
12				12
13				13
14				14
15				15
16				16
17				17
18				18
19				19
20				20
21				21
22				22
23				23
24				24
25				25
26				26
27				27
28				28
29				29
30				30
31				31
32				32
33				33
34				34
35				35
36				36

(3)

Name _____

JOURNAL

	DESCRIPTION	DEBIT	CREDIT	
1				1
2				2
3				3
4				4
5				5
6				6
7				7
8				8
9				9
10				10
11				11
12				12
13				13
14				14
15				15
16				16
17				17
18				18
19				19
20				20
21				21
22				22
23				23
24				24
25				25
26				26
27				27
28				28
29				29
30				30
31				31
32				32
33				33
34				34
35				35
36				36

Page not used.

(1) _____

_____

_____

_____

_____

_____

_____

_____

_____

_____

_____

_____

_____

_____

_____

_____

_____

_____

_____

_____

_____

_____

_____

_____

_____

_____

_____

_____

_____

_____

_____

_____

_____

_____

_____

_____

_____

_____

PROBLEM 3–11, Concluded

(2)

JOURNAL

	DESCRIPTION	DEBIT	CREDIT	
1				1
2				2
3				3
4				4
5				5
6				6
7				7
8				8
9				9
10				10
11				11
12				12
13				13
14				14
15				15
16				16
17				17
18				18
19				19
20				20
21				21
22				22
23				23
24				24
25				25
26				26
27				27
28				28
29				29
30				30
31				31
32				32
33				33
34				34
35				35
36				36

Name _____

Name _____

(1), (2), and (3) _____

Name _____

(1)

(2), (3), and (4)

Schedule for Distribution of Service Department Costs—Direct Method

(1)

Schedule for Distribution of Service Department Costs—Sequential Method

(2)

(2)

(2)

Name _____

JOURNAL

	DESCRIPTION	DEBIT	CREDIT	
1				1
2				2
3				3
4				4
5				5
6				6
7				7
8				8
9				9
10				10
11				11
12				12
13				13
14				14
15				15
16				16
17				17
18				18
19				19
20				20
21				21
22				22
23				23
24				24
25				25
26				26
27				27
28				28
29				29
30				30
31				31
32				32
33				33
34				34
35				35
36				36

PROBLEM 4–8, Concluded

	DESCRIPTION	DEBIT	CREDIT	
1				1
2				2
3				3
4				4
5				5
6				6
7				7
8				8
9				9
10				10
11				11
12				12
13				13
14				14
15				15
16				16
17				17
18				18
19				19
20				20
21				21
22				22
23				23
24				24
25				25
26				26
27				27
28				28
29				29
30				30
31				31
32				32
33				33
34				34
35				35
36				36

(1), (3), and (4)

(2) Total cost of jobs:

Description	Job 101	Job 102	Job 103	Job 104	Job 105	Job 106	Total

(1) and (2)

(3)

JOURNAL

	DESCRIPTION	DEBIT	CREDIT	
1				1
2				2
3				3
4				4
5				5
6				6
7				7
8				8
9				9
10				10
11				11
12				12
13				13
14				14
15				15
16				16
17				17
18				18
19				19
20				20
21				21
22				22
23				23
24				24
25				25
26				26
27				27
28				28
29				29
30				30
31				31
32				32
33				33
34				34
35				35
36				36

(1)

(2)

JOURNAL

	DESCRIPTION	DEBIT	CREDIT	
1				1
2				2
3				3
4				4
5				5
6				6
7				7
8				8
9				9
10				10
11				11
12				12
13				13
14				14
15				15
16				16
17				17
18				18
19				19
20				20
21				21
22				22
23				23
24				24
25				25
26				26
27				27
28				28
29				29
30				30
31				31
32				32
33				33
34				34
35				35
36				36

Name _____

(1) and (2)

JOURNAL

PAGE _____

	DESCRIPTION	DEBIT	CREDIT	
1				1
2				2
3				3
4				4
5				5
6				6
7				7
8				8
9				9
10				10
11				11
12				12
13				13
14				14
15				15
16				16
17				17
18				18
19				19
20				20
21				21
22				22
23				23
24				24
25				25
26				26
27				27
28				28
29				29
30				30
31				31
32				32
33				33
34				34
35				35
36				36

PROBLEM 4–13, Concluded

(2)

(1)

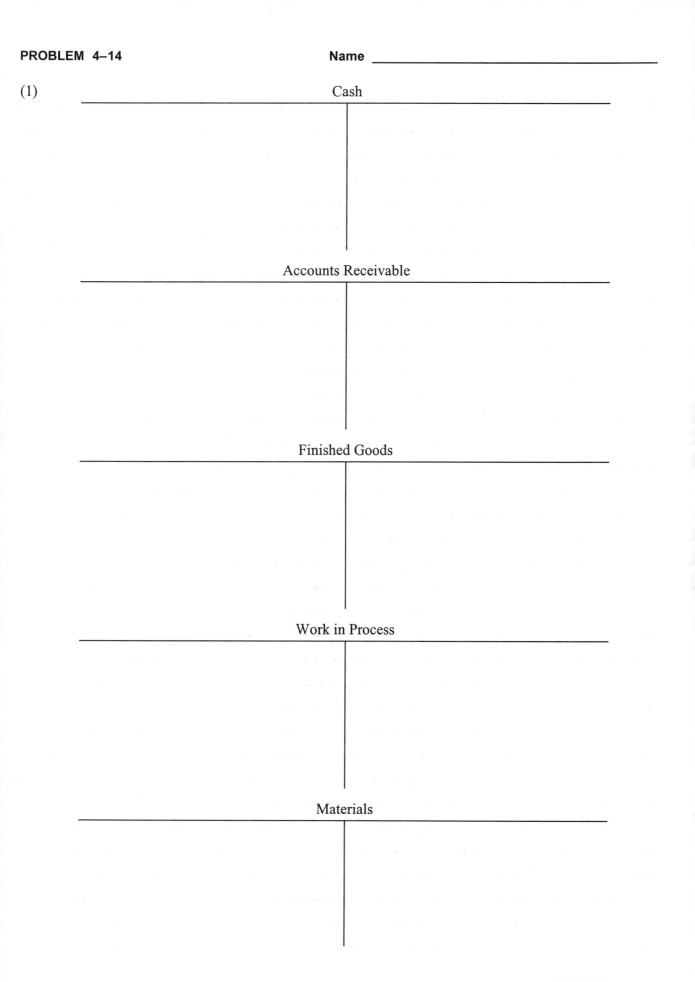

Cash

Accounts Receivable

Finished Goods

Work in Process

Materials

Prepaid Insurance

Factory Building

Accumulated Depreciation—Factory Building

Machinery & Equipment

Accumulated Depreciation—Machinery & Equipment

Office Equipment

Name _____

Accumulated Depreciation—Office Equipment

Accounts Payable

FICA Tax Payable

Federal Unemployment Tax Payable

State Unemployment Tax Payable

Employees Income Tax Payable

Wages Payable

Capital Stock

Retained Earnings

Factory Overhead

Factory Overhead—Stamping

Factory Overhead—Plating

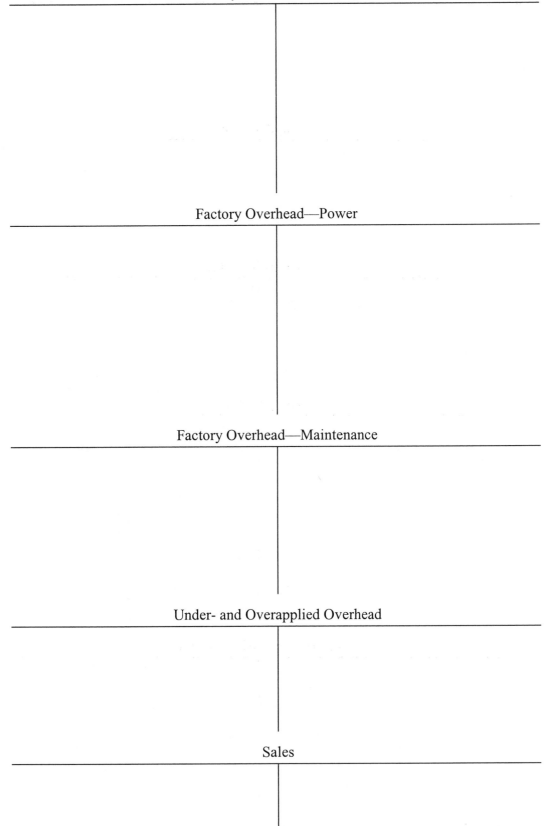

Factory Overhead—Power

Factory Overhead—Maintenance

Under- and Overapplied Overhead

Sales

Cost of Goods Sold

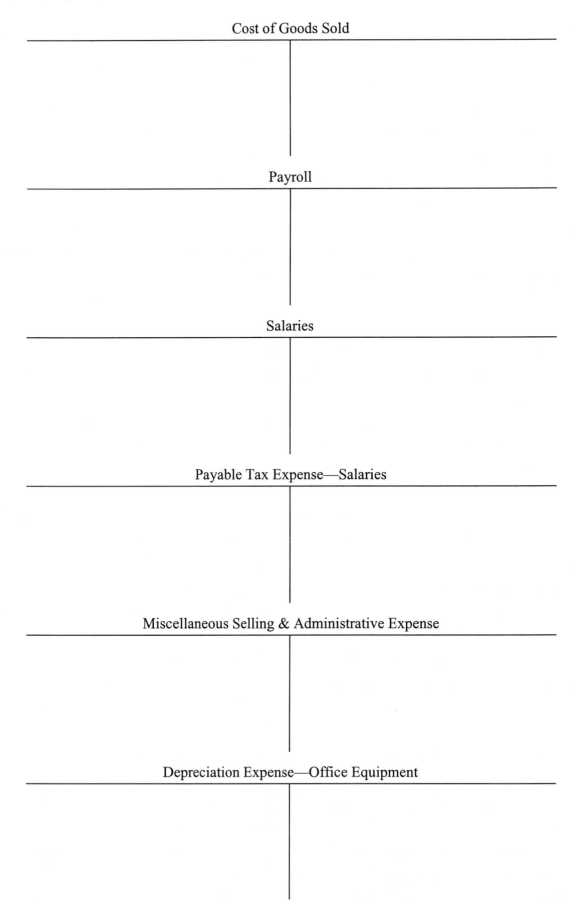

Payroll

Salaries

Payable Tax Expense—Salaries

Miscellaneous Selling & Administrative Expense

Depreciation Expense—Office Equipment

(2) Material Inventory Ledger Cards

(3) Job Cost Sheets

Name _____

(4)

JOURNAL

PAGE

	DESCRIPTION	DEBIT	CREDIT	
1				1
2				2
3				3
4				4
5				5
6				6
7				7
8				8
9				9
10				10
11				11
12				12
13				13
14				14
15				15
16				16
17				17
18				18
19				19
20				20
21				21
22				22
23				23
24				24
25				25
26				26
27				27
28				28
29				29
30				30
31				31
32				32
33				33
34				34
35				35
36				36

PROBLEM 4-14, Continued

PAGE

	DESCRIPTION	DEBIT	CREDIT	
1				1
2				2
3				3
4				4
5				5
6				6
7				7
8				8
9				9
10				10
11				11
12				12
13				13
14				14
15				15
16				16
17				17
18				18
19				19
20				20
21				21
22				22
23				23
24				24
25				25
26				26
27				27
28				28
29				29
30				30
31				31
32				32
33				33
34				34
35				35
36				36

Name _____

JOURNAL

PAGE

	DESCRIPTION	DEBIT	CREDIT	
1				1
2				2
3				3
4				4
5				5
6				6
7				7
8				8
9				9
10				10
11				11
12				12
13				13
14				14
15				15
16				16
17				17
18				18
19				19
20				20
21				21
22				22
23				23
24				24
25				25
26				26
27				27
28				28
29				29
30				30
31				31
32				32
33				33
34				34
35				35
36				36

Service Department Expense Distribution Work Sheet

For the Month Ended October 31, 2002

Description	Maintenance	Power	Stamping	Plating	Total

(5)

(6)(a)

(6)(b)

Custom Chrome Company

Statement of Cost of Goods Manufactured

For the Month Ended October 31, 2002

Custom Chrome Company

Income Statement

For the Month Ended October 31, 2002

Custom Chrome Company

Balance Sheet

October 31, 2002

Name _____

Stevens Products Co.

Cost of Production Summary

For the Month Ended February 28, 20--

George Company

Cost of Production Summary

For the Month Ended October 31, 20--

Name _____

Goode Manufacturing Co.

Cost of Production Summary—Cutting

For the Month Ended July 31, 2002

Goode Manufacturing Co.

Cost of Production Summary—Shaping

For the Month Ended July 31, 2002

Goode Manufacturing Co.

Cost of Production Summary—Finishing

For the Month Ended July 31, 2002

(1)

JOURNAL

	DESCRIPTION	DEBIT	CREDIT	
1				1
2				2
3				3
4				4
5				5
6				6
7				7
8				8
9				9
10				10
11				11
12				12
13				13
14				14
15				15
16				16
17				17
18				18
19				19
20				20
21				21
22				22
23				23
24				24
25				25
26				26
27				27
28				28
29				29
30				30
31				31
32				32
33				33
34				34
35				35
36				36

(2)

Goode Manufacturing Co.

Statement of Cost of Goods Manufactured

For the Month Ended July 31, 2002

Units	Unit Cost	Cost from Mixing Dept.	Costs in Cooking Dept.			Total Cost
			Materials	Labor	Factory Overhead	

Name _____

Irwin Corporation

Cost of Production Summary—Cutting

For the Month Ended May 31, 20--

Name _____

Irwin Corporation

Cost of Production Summary—Grinding

For the Month Ended May 31, 20--

Burton Manufacturing Co.

Cost of Production Summary—Forming

For the Month Ended March 31, 20--

Computations:

_____

_____

_____

_____

_____

_____

_____

_____

_____

_____

_____

_____

_____

_____

_____

_____

_____

_____

_____

_____

_____

_____

_____

_____

_____

_____

_____

_____

_____

_____

_____

_____

_____

_____

_____

_____

_____

_____

_____

_____

Page not used.

Name _____

(1)   San Marcos Manufacturing Co.

Cost of Production Summary—Mixing

For the Month Ended December 31, 20--

San Marcos Manufacturing Co.

Cost of Production Summary—Blending

For the Month Ended December 31, 20--

Name _____

San Marcos Manufacturing Co.

Cost of Production Summary—Bottling

For the Month Ended December 31, 20--

Name _____

(2)

San Marcos Manufacturing Co.

Departmental Cost Work Sheet

For the Month Ended December 31, 20--

Analysis	Cost per Unit Transf.	Units Received in Dept.	Units Transf. or on Hand	Amount Charged to Dept.	Amount Credited to Dept.

Analysis	Cost per Unit Transf.	Units Received in Dept.	Units Transf. or on Hand	Amount Charged to Dept.	Amount Credited to Dept.

PROBLEM 5–8, Continued

Summary:

	Amount	Total

(3)

JOURNAL

	DESCRIPTION	DEBIT	CREDIT	
1				1
2				2
3				3
4				4
5				5
6				6
7				7
8				8
9				9
10				10
11				11
12				12
13				13
14				14
15				15
16				16
17				17
18				18
19				19
20				20
21				21
22				22
23				23
24				24
25				25
26				26
27				27
28				28
29				29
30				30
31				31
32				32
33				33
34				34
35				35
36				36

(4)

San Marcos Manufacturing Co.

Statement of Cost of Goods Manufactured

For the Month Ended December 31, 20--

(1)   Lynx Manufacturing Co.

Cost of Production Summary—Mixing Dept.

For the Month Ended January 31, 20--

Lynx Manufacturing Co.

Cost of Production Summary—Mixing Dept.

For the Month Ended February 28, 20--

(2)

JOURNAL

	DESCRIPTION	DEBIT	CREDIT	
1				1
2				2
3				3
4				4
5				5
6				6
7				7
8				8
9				9
10				10
11				11
12				12
13				13
14				14
15				15
16				16
17				17
18				18
19				19
20				20
21				21
22				22
23				23
24				24
25				25
26				26
27				27
28				28
29				29
30				30
31				31
32				32
33				33
34				34
35				35
36				36

Name _____

JOURNAL

PAGE

	DESCRIPTION	DEBIT	CREDIT	
1				1
2				2
3				3
4				4
5				5
6				6
7				7
8				8
9				9
10				10
11				11
12				12
13				13
14				14
15				15
16				16
17				17
18				18
19				19
20				20
21				21
22				22
23				23
24				24
25				25
26				26
27				27
28				28
29				29
30				30
31				31
32				32
33				33
34				34
35				35
36				36

(1)   Columbus Manufacturing Co.

Cost of Production Summary—Dept. 1

For the Month Ended January 31, 20--

Columbus Manufacturing Co.

Cost of Production Summary—Dept. 2

For the Month Ended January 31, 20--

Name _____

Columbus Manufacturing Co.

Cost of Production Summary—Dept. 3

For the Month Ended January 31, 20--

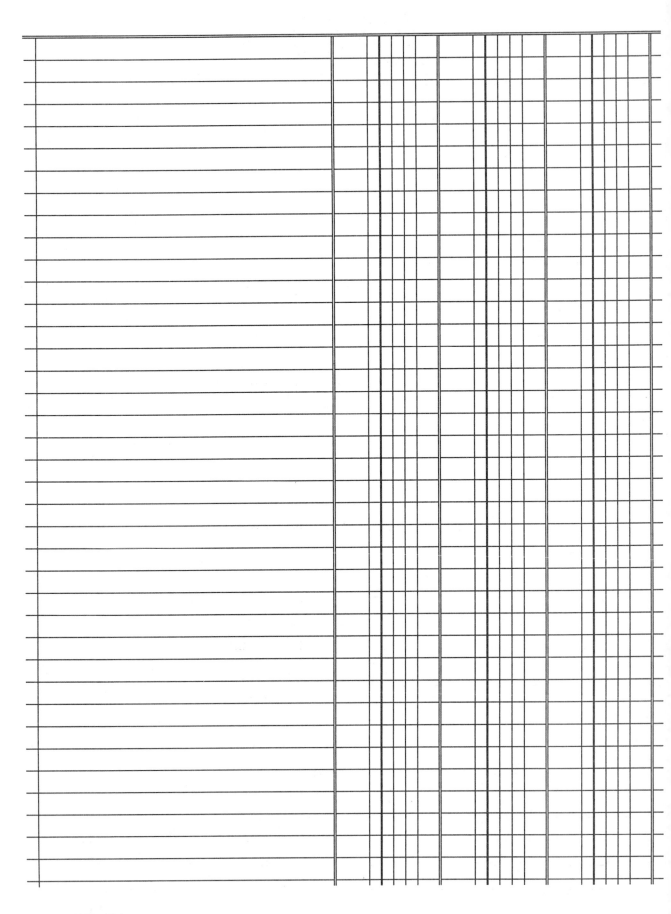

(2)

Columbus Manufacturing Co.

Departmental Cost Work Sheet

For the Month Ended January 31, 20--

Analysis	Cost per Unit Transf.	Units Received in Dept.	Units Transf. or on Hand	Amount Charged to Dept.	Amount Credited to Dept.

Analysis	Cost per Unit Transf.	Units Received in Dept.	Units Transf. or on Hand	Amount Charged to Dept.	Amount Credited to Dept.

PROBLEM 6–3, Continued

Name _____

Summary: | Amount | Total

PROBLEM 6–3, Continued

(3)

JOURNAL

	DESCRIPTION	DEBIT	CREDIT	
1				1
2				2
3				3
4				4
5				5
6				6
7				7
8				8
9				9
10				10
11				11
12				12
13				13
14				14
15				15
16				16
17				17
18				18
19				19
20				20
21				21
22				22
23				23
24				24
25				25
26				26
27				27
28				28
29				29
30				30
31				31
32				32
33				33
34				34
35				35
36				36

(4)   Columbus Manufacturing Co.

                 Cost of Production Summary—Dept. 1

                 For the Month Ended January 31, 20--

(1) and (2) _____

_____

_____

_____

_____

_____

_____

_____

_____

_____

_____

_____

_____

_____

_____

_____

_____

_____

_____

_____

_____

_____

_____

_____

_____

_____

_____

_____

_____

_____

_____

_____

_____

_____

_____

_____

_____

_____

_____

Name _____

Zenith Products Co.

Cost of Production Summary

For the Month Ended October 31, 20--

Page not used.

Name _____

Charlie Manufacturing Co.

Cost of Production Summary—Dept. A

For the Month Ended May 31, 20--

Name _____

Charlie Manufacturing Co.

Cost of Production Summary—Dept. B

For the Month Ended May 31, 20--

Buckner Products Co.

Cost of Production Summary

For the Month Ended October 31, 20--

(1)

(2)

Name _____ WP–193

Name _____

Name _____

Mars Production Company

Cost of Production Summary—Machining Department

For the Month Ended July 31, 20--

Mars Production Company

Cost of Production Summary—Finishing Department

For the Month Ended July 31, 20--

(1) Materials Price and Quantity Variances:

PROBLEM 7–1, Concluded

(2) Labor Rate and Efficiency Variances:

Name _____

(1) and (3)

(2) and (4)

(1) and (3)

(2) and (4)

(1), (2), and (5)

PROBLEM 7–4, Concluded

(3), (4), and (6)

(4), (5), and (6)

Labor:

Materials quantity variance:

_____
_____
_____
_____
_____
_____
_____
_____
_____
_____
_____
_____
_____
_____
_____
_____
_____
_____
_____
_____

Materials purchase price variance:

_____
_____
_____
_____
_____
_____
_____
_____
_____
_____
_____
_____
_____
_____
_____
_____
_____

PROBLEM 7-6, Concluded

Labor efficiency variance:

_____

_____

_____

_____

_____

_____

_____

_____

_____

_____

_____

_____

_____

_____

_____

_____

_____

Labor rate variance:

_____

_____

_____

_____

_____

_____

_____

_____

_____

_____

_____

_____

_____

_____

_____

_____

(1) and (2)

(3)   Ending Work in Process
_____

_____

_____

_____

_____

_____

_____

_____

_____

(4)

(1) and (2)

JOURNAL

PAGE _____

	DESCRIPTION	DEBIT	CREDIT	
1				1
2				2
3				3
4				4
5				5
6				6
7				7
8				8
9				9
10				10
11				11
12				12
13				13
14				14
15				15
16				16
17				17
18				18
19				19
20				20
21				21
22				22
23				23
24				24
25				25
26				26
27				27
28				28
29				29
30				30
31				31
32				32
33				33
34				34
35				35
36				36

(1)–(4)

PROBLEM 7-9, Concluded

(1) Calculation of Net Variances

	Mixing			Blending			Total		
	Equivalent production of 7,000 units			Equivalent production of 5,500 units					
	Standard Cost	Actual Cost	Fav. (Unfav.) Variance	Standard Cost	Actual Cost	Fav. (Unfav.) Variance	Standard Cost	Actual Cost	Fav. (Unfav.) Variance
Materials:									
Labor:									
Factory Overhead:									
Total									

(2)

Name _____

PROBLEM 7–10, Continued

(3)

JOURNAL   PAGE

	DESCRIPTION	DEBIT	CREDIT	
1				1
2				2
3				3
4				4
5				5
6				6
7				7
8				8
9				9
10				10
11				11
12				12
13				13
14				14
15				15
16				16
17				17
18				18
19				19
20				20
21				21
22				22
23				23
24				24
25				25
26				26
27				27
28				28
29				29
30				30
31				31
32				32
33				33
34				34
35				35
36				36

WP–224

Name _____

(4)

	Mixing	Blending

PROBLEM 7-10, Concluded

(5)

	Mixing	Blending	Total

(6)

(1)   Glide-Rite Tire Company

Sales Budget

For the Year Ended December 31, 2002

Product	Unit Sales Volume	Unit Selling Price	Total Sales

(2)   Glide-Rite Tire Company

Production Budget

For the Year Ended December 31, 2002

Glide-Rite Tire Company

Direct Materials Budget

For the Year Ended January 31, 2002

Name _____

Glide-Rite Tire Company

Direct Labor Budget

For the Year Ended January 31, 2002

PROBLEM 8–1, Concluded

Glide-Rite Tire Company

Factory Overhead Budget

For the Year Ended December 31, 2002

Glide-Rite Tire Company

Cost of Goods Sold Budget

For the Year Ended December 31, 2002

Name _____

(1)

Glide-Rite Tire Company
Selling and Administrative Expenses Budget
For the Year Ended December 31, 2002

PROBLEM 8–2, Concluded

(2)

Glide-Rite Tire Company

Budgeted Income Statement

For the Year Ended December 31, 2002

(1)   Factory Overhead Cost Budget

Percent of normal capacity.....................................   80%   90%   110%

(2)   Factory Overhead Cost Budget

Percent of normal capacity 80%   90%   110%

(3) and (4)

(1), (2), and (3) _____

(4), (5), and (6)

(1)

JOURNAL

	DESCRIPTION	DEBIT	CREDIT	
1				1
2				2
3				3
4				4
5				5
6				6
7				7
8				8
9				9
10				10
11				11
12				12
13				13
14				14
15				15
16				16
17				17
18				18
19				19
20				20
21				21
22				22
23				23
24				24
25				25
26				26
27				27
28				28
29				29
30				30
31				31
32				32
33				33
34				34
35				35
36				36

JOURNAL

PAGE

	DESCRIPTION	DEBIT	CREDIT	
1				1
2				2
3				3
4				4
5				5
6				6
7				7
8				8
9				9
10				10
11				11
12				12
13				13
14				14
15				15
16				16
17				17
18				18
19				19
20				20
21				21
22				22
23				23
24				24
25				25
26				26
27				27
28				28
29				29
30				30
31				31
32				32
33				33
34				34
35				35
36				36

Variances are calculated as follows:

<u>Materials</u>

Variances are calculated as follows:

<u>Labor</u>

Variances are calculated as follows:

<u>Factory Overhead</u>

PROBLEM 8-7, Concluded

(2)

(3)

(1)   Standard Cost of Production for October

_____

_____

_____

_____

_____

_____

_____

_____

_____

_____

_____

_____

_____

_____

_____

_____

_____

_____

(2)   Schedule Computing Materials Price Variance

_____

_____

_____

_____

_____

_____

_____

_____

_____

_____

_____

_____

_____

_____

_____

(3)   Schedule of Materials and Labor Variances for October

	Lot 30	Lot 31	Lot 32	Total

(4)   Schedule of Overhead Variances for October

Name _____

PROBLEM 8–9, Concluded

(1) _____

PROBLEM 8-10 (Appendix), Concluded

(2)

(1)

(2)

Schedule of Variances from Standard Cost for December

Three-Variance Method

Name _____

(1)
_____

_____

_____

_____

_____

_____

_____

_____

_____

_____

_____

_____

_____

_____

_____

_____

_____

_____

_____

_____

_____

_____

_____

_____

_____

_____

_____

_____

_____

_____

_____

_____

_____

_____

_____

_____

_____

(2) and (3)

(4)

Cooney and Tesch

Attorneys-at-Law

Summary of Engagement Account

(1)   Cost Performance Report

_____

_____

_____

_____

_____

_____

_____

_____

_____

_____

_____

_____

_____

_____

_____

_____

_____

_____

_____

_____

_____

_____

_____

_____

_____

_____

_____

_____

_____

_____

_____

_____

_____

_____

_____

_____

_____

_____

(2)

(2)

Chatfield and Griffin

Professional Labor Budget

For the Year Ended December 31, 2002

(1)

Chatfield and Griffin

Overhead Budget

For the Year Ended December 31, 2002

(2)

Chatfield and Griffin

Other Expenses Budget

For the Year Ended December 31, 2002

(3)

Chatfield and Griffin

Budgeted Income Statement

For the Year Ended December 31, 2002

(1) and (2)

PROBLEM 9–6, Concluded

Page not used.

Williams Manufacturing Co.
Income Statement
For the Month Ended March 31, 2002

	(1) Absorption Costing	(2) Direct Costing

Williams Manufacturing Co.

Income Statement

For the Month Ended April 30, 2002

	(1) Absorption Costing	(2) Direct Costing

Name _____

(1) Household Manufacturing Company

Income Statement by Territory

Name _____

(1)

Silicon Manufacturing Company
Territory and Company Income Statements
For the Year Ended December 31, 2002

(2)

(1)   North-Eastern Publishing Company

Professional Division: Product and Divisional Income Statements

For the Year Ended December 31, 2002

(2)

North-Eastern Publishing Company

Professional Division

Market Income Statements: Accounting Books

For the Year Ended December 31, 2002

(3)

(1) and (3)

(2)

Daveeda Manufacturing Company

Income Statement

For the Year Ended December 31, 2002

(1) and (2) _____

(3)(a)

Giganto Company

Absorption Costing Income Statement

For the Year Ended December 31, 2002

(3)(b)　　　　　　　　　　　　Giganto Company

Direct Costing Income Statement

For the Year Ended December 31, 2002

(2)

(3)

(4) and (5)

(1) – (3) _____

_____

_____

_____

_____

_____

_____

_____

_____

_____

_____

_____

_____

_____

_____

_____

_____

_____

_____

_____

_____

_____

_____

_____

_____

_____

_____

_____

_____

_____

_____

_____

_____

_____

_____

_____

_____

PROBLEM 10–8, Concluded

(4) - (6)

(1)

(1) and (2) _____

_____

_____

_____

_____

_____

_____

_____

_____

_____

_____

_____

_____

_____

_____

_____

_____

_____

_____

_____

_____

_____

_____

_____

_____

_____

_____

_____

_____

_____

_____

_____

_____

_____

_____

_____

_____

_____

_____

(3) and (4)

(1) _____

(2)

(1) _____

_____

_____

_____

_____

_____

_____

_____

_____

_____

_____

_____

_____

_____

_____

_____

_____

_____

_____

_____

_____

_____

_____

_____

_____

_____

_____

_____

_____

_____

_____

_____

_____

_____

_____

_____

(2)